# Two's Cooking
## Jane and Jeremy Strode

First published 2005 in Australia
by Pan Macmillan Australia Pty Limited
St Martins Tower, 31 Market Street, Sydney

National Library of Australia
Cataloguing-in-Publication data:

Strode, Jeremy.
  Two's cooking.
  ISBN 1 40503686 9.
  1. Cookery. I. Strode, Jane. II. Title.
641.5

Photography by Karl Schwerdtfeger
Designed by Andrew Ashton and Marco Gjergja,
Studio Pip and Co. Melbourne
Printed by Imago Productions (F.E.) Pte. Ltd.

MACMILLAN
Pan Macmillan Australia

# Food brought us together.

Food brought us together. We met in 2000 while working in the kitchens of Langton's Restaurant and Wine Bar in Melbourne. Food is our passion. We spend most of our time either cooking food, eating food or talking food. We married in March 2004. When not eating in other restaurants, our days off are regularly spent cooking the food you'll find in this book.

Working all day in kitchens is long and tiring. The pleasure we derive from creating, cooking and eating great food is the reason we do what we do. Even after a hard day's work we look forward to cooking dinner for one another – we come from extremely different cooking backgrounds and we're still sharing ideas and techniques. Whoever gets the night off cooking gets to do the dishes!

Our busy lives can make us forget how special a well-cooked meal at home can be. Making the effort to shop for fresh ingredients for even the most simple of dishes is so rewarding. It may be a cliché, but we think the simple things done well really are the best. We encourage you to buy the best produce available within your budget. For example, it's important to us to have proper sea salt, good olive oil and a decent vinegar in our pantry. We are passionate about buying seasonal fruit and vegetables at their best from local grocers or a market. Try to buy meat free from growth hormones and antibiotics, and poultry that is *certified* free-range, from a reputable butcher.

Also try to buy fresh fish that is not endangered or in short supply. It's these things that make the difference between an okay meal and a great one.

When creating this book, we decided to base our recipes around the rhythms of the week. Simple food for relaxed Sundays; quick, tasty one-course meals to get you through the week; and more sophisticated offerings for weekends. The Friday recipes take a little more time and planning and are perfect for when you want to have a couple of friends over. The Saturday recipes are the most involved and perfect for special occasions. We have written four-course dinner-party menus for each of the seasons and included advice on planning your menu.

On page 180, you'll find a glossary of techniques, ingredients and equipment you may not be sure about. The most important pieces of equipment you will ever need are sharp knifes.

Last but not least, we encourage you to make this book your own. Once you feel comfortable with each recipe, improvise and experiment – that way your own skills and knowledge will evolve. These recipes are part of our lives. We hope this book will become part of your life, too.

**Jane and Jeremy**

# Thanks.

## For Max and Hunter.

We would like to thank Alex Craig and everyone at Pan Macmillan; Karl Schwerdtfeger; Andrew Ashton from Pip and Co.; Keith Shreeve and Kin Chen from The Wall Café – Sydney; Dave Sharry and Margo Collins from Wall Two 80 Café – Melbourne; Sous Chef Chris Coolahan and the Team; Patrick Ryan and staff at the Republic Hotel – Sydney; Lorraine Godsmark, George Sinclair and everyone at Yellow Bistro and Food Store – Sydney; Julian Sefton; Rob Barbera from Flying Squid Café – Sydney; Lisa Featherby; Magda Ching; Max Strode; Justine Topfer; Karel Syme; Madeline Smith; Caris Haughan; Paul McCarthy; Ben Allen; Anthony Puharich from Vic's Premium Quality Meats; Demcos Seafoods; Joto Fresh Fish; Ian Lind at Fishy Biz; Matt Brown's Greens; Fratelli Fresh; Simon Johnsons; Essential Ingredient; Hale Imports; and Ronda, John and Lucinda Booth.

# What's inside.

## School nights.

38

## Fridays for four.

# 112

## Big night in.

# 136

# Sunday again.

As Sunday guarantees both of us a day off, we try and keep whatever we do as relaxed as possible, be it a coffee and pide at the Wall Café in Sydney or a casual barbecue as a way to catch up with friends. Sometimes we may even treat ourselves to a cooked breakfast at home. If a major sleep-in is required, then an afternoon tea will fit the bill. Whatever we end up doing, we are always glad that it's Sunday again.

## Tomato Jam

Heat the oil in a large, heavy-based saucepan over medium-low heat. Add onion and garlic, season well, and cook until onion is soft.

Meanwhile, pass tomatoes through a vegetable mouli to remove any skin and seeds. Add tomatoes, sugar, vinegar and bay leaf to the saucepan. Bring to the boil, then simmer over a medium heat, stirring occasionally, until mixture begins to thicken.

Reduce heat to low. Cook mixture, stirring regularly to prevent it sticking to pan, for 2 minutes or until tomatoes are thick and shiny and the oil begins to sit on the top. Remove from heat and set aside to cool.

Pour into a clean container or sterilised glass jar and refrigerate.

This is my favourite thing to have on hand and I love to give it as a gift at Christmas. It needs a little time and attention to get the best results, but it is well worth it. Tomato Jam complements almost everything – sandwiches, burgers, avocado on toast, grilled meats, eggs, fishcakes. A couple of tablespoons added to any tomato-based sauce will give it a boost. It lasts for weeks in the fridge, but is usually gobbled up within days. Jane.

**Makes 1½L**

200ml olive oil

1 medium brown onion, finely chopped

3 cloves garlic, finely chopped

sea salt

freshly ground white pepper

4 x 810g cans whole tomatoes

250g white sugar

200ml red-wine vinegar

1 bay leaf

## Banana and Honey Jam

Place all ingredients in a heavy-based saucepan. Warm gently over low heat, stirring, until sugar dissolves. Increase heat and bring to the boil. Reduce heat, bring to a simmer, and stir continuously with a flat-bottomed spoon until jam reaches 105°C on a sugar thermometer. Jam should be a deep purple. Remove from heat and set aside to cool.

Pour into a clean container or a sterilised glass jar and refrigerate.

If you ever have too many over-ripening bananas, this is an excellent way of using them up. Bananas and honey are a winning combination and the structure of honey stops this jam from crystallising. It catches easily while cooking, so you need to keep stirring. It is particularly good on crumpets and will last for up to 6 weeks in the fridge, and longer if you store the jam in a sterilised jar and then simmer the jar in water for 40 minutes. Jane.

**Makes 400g**

500g ripe bananas, peeled and mashed

250g honey

100g caster sugar

1 lime, juiced and strained

## Dried-Fruit Compote

Bring 800ml water and sugar to the boil in a large saucepan. Add remaining ingredients and simmer gently for 15 minutes.

Remove from heat, cover and set aside to cool, then refrigerate overnight.

Store in a clean container or sterilised glass jar in the fridge.

We first started making this compote to put on the breakfast menu at Langton's Restaurant and Wine Bar in Melbourne. It was served with porridge or granola, but I love eating it with just a huge dollop of good-quality sheep's-milk yoghurt. It's also wonderful with pancakes or French toast. Dried fruit (especially prunes) is full of natural fibre and a great source of antioxidants, so this compote is a healthy addition to your diet. It will keep for at least a month. Jane.

**Makes about 1½L**

200g sugar
1 vanilla bean, split and scraped
1 cinnamon stick
1 clove
rind and juice of 1 orange
150g dried pears
150g dried apples
100g prunes
100g dried apricots

## Sweet Potato, Pea and Oregano Frittata

Preheat oven to 180°C. Whisk eggs and cream thoroughly. Melt butter in a small, non-stick ovenproof frying pan over medium heat. Add onion and sweat until soft. Add sweet potato, peas and oregano, season, add egg mixture and cook, stirring, for 1 minute.

Place frying pan in oven and cook for 20 minutes or until just set and centre puffs up. Remove from oven and turn pan upside down to remove frittata.

Cut into 4 pieces and serve with salad leaves and Tomato Jam (see recipe on page 10).

Frittatas are simple and tasty, and they can be made with any number of ingredients. Our other favourite additions are capsicum and goat's cheese, or bacon, onion and spinach. This is a great meal when you are short on time and have bits and pieces to use up in the fridge. We often make frittata for staff dinners if we are having a particularly busy day in the restaurant and are pushed for time. It is surprisingly filling. Jane.

**To serve four people**

4 free-range eggs

100ml cream (35% fat content)

40g unsalted butter

½ Spanish onion, finely chopped

1 small sweet potato, peeled, diced, roasted

½ cup peas

3 sprigs oregano, leaves picked

sea salt

freshly ground white pepper

## Fried Eggs, Sausages and White Bean Stew

To make White Bean Stew, boil the beans in water for 30 minutes or until three-quarters cooked. Meanwhile, heat a heavy-based saucepan over medium-low heat, add the oil, onion and garlic and sweat until soft. Add bacon and sweat for another 5 minutes. Add wine and cook until reduced by three-quarters. Add tomatoes, stock, bay leaf and thyme, season and simmer gently for about 30 minutes.

Strain beans and add to stew with sugar. Simmer gently, stirring regularly, for a further 30 minutes or until beans are very soft. Season to taste, remove from heat and set aside.

Preheat oven to 200°C. Prick sausages, place on a tray and cook in oven for about 15 minutes. Reheat 2 portions of White Bean Stew. Melt the butter in a non-stick frying pan over a low heat. Crack eggs into pan and cook gently until white just sets, then season.

Place the beans to one side of 2 plates and an egg alongside. Place sausages on top of beans and serve.

I don't usually eat the 'full Monty' at breakfast, but occasionally it's nearer lunchtime and hunger demands something rich and hearty. The White Bean Stew is a really tasty accompaniment that keeps in the fridge for a week. Make sure you buy sausages from a reputable butcher. Jeremy.

**To serve two people**

4 veal-and-pork sausages

30g unsalted butter

2 free-range eggs

sea salt

freshly ground white pepper

**White Bean Stew**

60g dried cannellini beans,
   soaked in water overnight

80ml olive oil

1 brown onion, peeled
   and finely chopped

2 cloves garlic, peeled
   and finely chopped

2 rashers of bacon,
   diced into ½cm pieces

150ml red wine

250g crushed canned tomatoes

150ml veal stock

1 bay leaf

2 sprigs thyme

sea salt

freshly ground white pepper

1 teaspoon sugar

## Roast Beetroot, Pine Nut and Parsley Salad with Onion Dressing

Preheat oven to 180°C. Place beetroots on a roasting tray and bake for 1–1½ hours or until tender. Pierce with a skewer or small knife to test. Remove from oven and set aside to cool. Peel with a small knife and cut into wedges.

To make Onion Dressing, warm olive oil in a saucepan on medium-low heat and add onion. Season well and sweat for 20 minutes or until very soft. Remove from heat, add vinegar and allow onions to soak up vinegar.

Dice eggplant into 2cm pieces, toss with salt and set aside for 20 minutes. Rinse and pat dry with paper towel. Heat olive oil in a frying pan over medium-high heat and shallow-fry eggplant until golden brown. Drain on paper towel.

Place beetroot, eggplant, parsley, pine nuts and Onion Dressing in a large bowl. Season and toss to combine.

Serve on 4 plates, or in a large salad bowl, and top with teaspoons of goat's curd.

The difference in this salad is that it's rich, and the only leaves used are parsley. We use Onion Dressing on many other salads – it has a full-bodied flavour, due to the onions being sweated for a long time. The earthiness of the beetroots perfectly matches the acid in the goat's cheese. Jane.

**To serve four people**

4 large beetroots

1 large eggplant

sea salt

olive oil, for shallow frying

1 cup flat-leaf parsley, leaves picked and washed

50g pine nuts, toasted

freshly ground white pepper

100g fresh goat's curd

**Onion Dressing**

200ml olive oil

1 medium brown onion, finely diced

50ml balsamic vinegar

## Ham, Egg, Tomato and Rocket Pide

Spread bases of bread with mayonnaise and top
with ham, tomato, egg and rocket. Spread the other
2 slices with mustard and place on top.

Push down lightly and toast in a sandwich-maker
or under a grill.

Cut in half and serve.

We first ate this delicious pide at the Wall Two 80 Café
in Melbourne. It quickly became our weekend staple,
especially after a late Saturday night out. Luckily for
us, there is now a Wall Café in Sydney, so we can still
get our weekend fix. Jeremy.

**To serve two people**

2 slices turkish bread,
 sliced through the centre

mayonnaise

2 slices good-quality ham

2 roma tomatoes, sliced thinly

2 free-range eggs, hard-boiled
 and sliced

1 handful rocket, washed
 and leaves picked

grain mustard

## Fennel and Blue Cheese Tart

Gently roll out pastry to ½cm thickness. Line a 23cm tart shell with pastry. Wrap well with cling film and rest in the fridge for at least 30 minutes.

Preheat oven to 160°C. Place a little olive oil and fennel on an oven tray and roast for 30 minutes or until golden brown and soft.

Line pastry shell with foil and top with some uncooked rice. Blind bake for 20 minutes or until golden brown. Remove foil and rice and return to oven until pastry is an even brown colour. Brush pastry with egg yolk to seal. Return to oven for 2 minutes.

Lay fennel over pastry and crumble over blue cheese. Whisk together cream and eggs, season and pour onto tart, filling to the top. Bake for 30 minutes or until golden brown and just set in the centre.

Remove tart from shell and set aside on a wire rack to allow steam to escape and keep pastry crisp.

Cut into 6 slices and serve with mixed salad leaves.

This first appeared on the menu at Langton's Restaurant and Wine Bar in Melbourne. As we bake our tarts fresh every day, we would eat the leftovers. It quickly became a favourite snack. Gorgonzola would be the perfect cheese. When dealing with pastry, the longer the resting time the better (overnight is best), as this helps to prevent shrinkage when baking. In the restaurant we always prepare at least a day ahead and often have tart shells lined in advance and kept in the freezer. Pastry freezes well and, once frozen, will not oxidise – exposure to the air turns pastry brown after a period of time. Jeremy.

### To serve six people

300g savoury shortcrust pastry

olive oil

2 bulbs fennel, trimmed and
   cut into 1cm wedges

1 egg yolk

150g blue cheese

400ml cream (35% fat content)

3 free-range eggs

sea salt

freshly ground white pepper

## Sardines and Soured Onions on Toast

To make Soured Onions, place onions and olive oil in a saucepan and cook slowly over low heat until onions start to soften. Add other ingredients, season and cook gently until onions are soft. Set aside to marinate.

Brush both sides of sourdough slices with olive oil and toast on an open grill or barbecue.

Heat a non-stick frying pan over low heat and add a little olive oil. Gently cook the sardines on both sides. Place sardines on top of bread and drizzle with Soured Onions and their juices.

Garnish with a salad of parsley and watercress.

The soured onions idea came from some antipasti I once ate in Venice. Their sharpness against the oiliness of the sardines works really well. Forum cabernet vinegar is an exceptional product, but if you can't get your hands on it then use the best-quality red-wine vinegar you can find. Jeremy.

**To serve four people**

4 large slices sourdough
olive oil
16 sardines, butterflied

**Soured Onions**

300g brown onions, shredded
300ml extra-virgin olive oil
3 sprigs thyme
2 bay leaves
12 black peppercorns
150ml Forum cabernet vinegar
sea salt
freshly ground white pepper

## Roast Spatchcock with Sour Cream Stuffing

Preheat oven to 140°C.

Melt butter in a frying pan over medium-low heat, add onion, celery and thyme leaves and season well. Cook for 12 minutes or until onion is soft. Drain on paper towel and place in a bowl.

With the crust left on, tear the bread roughly into pieces. Place in oven for 8–10 minutes or until dried out (a little bit of colour is good).

Add bread to onions and allow to cool. Stir through sour cream (using your hands if necessary) and season to taste.

Shape stuffing as best you can into 4 balls and push into cavity of each spatchcock. Tie legs together to keep stuffing from falling out.

Preheat oven to 200°C.

Heat a large ovenproof frying pan and add a little vegetable oil. Season birds well. Place birds in hot pan, breast side down, and cook for 2 minutes or until they colour.

Turn birds onto their backs and roast in oven for 30 minutes. Remove and transfer to a warm place (such as top of oven or on bench beside oven) to rest for at least 15 minutes.

Remove string from legs – or remove legs, breast and stuffing from cavity – and serve the birds whole. Accompany with roast vegetables, such as pumpkin and carrots, garnish with watercress and serve.

I have served this meal many times with chicken broth and corn cakes, but it is always the stuffing that people comment on. It can be used to stuff other poultry, such as chicken or turkey. Jane.

**To serve four people**

80g butter

2 small brown onions, finely chopped

2 celery sticks, finely chopped

8 sprigs thyme, leaves picked

sea salt

freshly ground white pepper

4 thick slices sourdough loaf

6 tablespoons sour cream

4 spatchcock, wishbone and wing tips removed

vegetable oil

## Barbecued Ocean Trout with Eggplant Relish

Sprinkle eggplant with table salt and set aside for 30 minutes.

Meanwhile, heat a little olive oil in a heavy-based saucepan over medium-low heat. Add onion, garlic and chilli, season well and cook until onions are very soft and starting to colour.

Wash eggplant and pat dry with paper towel. Add eggplant, sugar and vinegar to onions, increase heat to medium and cook, stirring, for 40 minutes or until eggplant is soft and liquid has reduced. Season to taste and set aside.

Heat barbecue until very hot. Brush ocean trout with olive oil and season. Cook, skin side down, for 4 minutes or until skin is crispy. Turn over and cook for a further 3 minutes, making sure trout is still pink in the middle.

Serve with a large spoonful of relish and accompany with other barbecued foods such as corn on the cob or foil-wrapped potatoes.

I'm a big fan of sweet-and-sour flavours, like this relish. Eggplant that is cooked for a long time becomes smooth and silky, so the texture of this relish has a great mouthfeel. It can be served with red or white meat, most fish and is fantastic with fried food. Jane.

**To serve two people**

2 x 200g fillets ocean trout, skin on

**Eggplant Relish**

2 medium eggplants, skin peeled and discarded, diced into 1cm pieces

table salt

olive oil

1 large brown onion, diced

2 garlic cloves, finely chopped

1 small red chilli, finely chopped

sea salt

freshly ground white pepper

100g brown sugar

100ml red-wine vinegar

## Barbecued Topside

Preheat barbecue to high.

Mix together all ingredients, except meat, in a bowl and season well.

Season topside and brown all over on the barbecue – this should take about 25 minutes. Reduce heat to low.

Lay 2 long lengths of heavy-duty foil on top of each other. Place half the sauce in the centre. Place meat on top and cover with remaining sauce. Seal foil and cook, seam side up, for 1½–2 hours or until meat is very tender.

Peel back foil, remove meat and cut into thin slices. Spoon over sauce and serve.

This recipe is adapted from an old recipe of my mother's. I have fond memories of standing around the barbecue waiting for the meat to be ready. The smell was amazing and my stomach was always rumbling loudly by the time the foil was being peeled off and the meat sliced up. Serve it with a mixed salad such as tomato and basil, or potatoes and salad leaves. Jane.

**To serve six people**

2 large brown onions, finely sliced
200ml tomato sauce
200ml tomato paste
2 garlic cloves, finely chopped
1 tablespoon Worcestershire sauce
2 tablespoons Dijon mustard
2 tablespoons white-wine vinegar
2 teaspoons Tabasco sauce
sea salt
freshly ground white pepper
1 x 2–2½kg piece topside beef

## Raspberry Turkish Delight

130g cornflour
250g icing sugar, sifted
125ml water

Mix together in large, heavy-based saucepan.

460g sugar

Dissolve sugar in ½ cup of water and heat to 115°C.

¼ teaspoon tartaric acid
1 tablespoon lemon juice

Mix together in a small bowl and add to sugar syrup once it has reached temperature.

Turkish Delight always seemed like such a mysterious treat, so discovering a recipe for it was especially satisfying. Raspberries give it a pink colour without using food colouring and the flavour is lovely. If you want a smooth result, puree and strain the raspberries before adding them, but I quite like the texture with the seeds left in. Strawberries make a good alternative, but the colour is less vibrant. You will need a pastry thermometer for this recipe. The layout of this recipe is different because you need to have four combinations of ingredients ready to go at the same time. I find this layout easiest to understand. Don't be discouraged – it's not as difficult as it looks and the result is impressive. Jane.

500ml boiling water

Add to the cornflour mixture with the sugar syrup at the same time.

Cook mixture on medium heat, stirring with a spatula to prevent it catching on the bottom, for 40 minutes or until thick and almost translucent.

10 leaves gelatin
1 cup raspberries
3 lemons, juiced and strained
rosewater

Soak gelatin in cold water until soft and stir into mixture. Stir through raspberries. Stir in lemon juice and rosewater to taste.

Line a 20 x 30cm tray with cling film or greaseproof paper and pour mixture into tray. Refrigerate overnight to set.

Turn out onto a chopping board and peel back film or paper. Dice into 1½cm pieces and dust with icing sugar before serving. If not serving immediately, store in refrigerator without dusting.

**Makes around 20 pieces**

130g cornflour

250g icing sugar, sifted

125ml water

460g sugar

½ cup of water

¼ teaspoon tartaric acid

1 tablespoon lemon juice

500ml boiling water

10 leaves gelatin

1 cup raspberries

3 lemons, juiced and strained

rosewater

## White Pan Forte

Preheat oven to 140°C. Line a 20 x 30cm baking tray with greaseproof paper and grease lightly.

Combine all dry ingredients, except sugar, in a large bowl. Place marzipan in a food processor and process until broken up.

Place sugar and honey in a saucepan with a small amount of water and dissolve over low heat. Bring to the boil and allow to reach 115°C, then pour over marzipan with food processor running and process to a smooth paste. Transfer to a large bowl. Stir through dry ingredients – you may need to use your hands.

Press into lined tray, wetting hands slightly if needed, place in oven and bake for 45 minutes.

Transfer to a wire rack to cool, then cut into 2cm squares with a serrated knife. Store in an airtight container.

Dust with icing sugar before serving.

Waking up in Siena, drinking an espresso and eating a piece of pan forte is like being in heaven. It was after a trip to Italy and much eating of many different types of pan forte that I set about writing a recipe for White Pan Forte, as I couldn't find one anywhere. I like mine spicy, so you may need to adjust the spice and pepper to your taste. Pan forte will last for at least a year in an airtight container in the cupboard. Jane.

**Makes 30 pieces**

500g mixed nuts, such as almonds, pine nuts, hazelnuts and pistachios

600g mixed dried fruit, such as mixed peel, apricots, cherries, pear, glacé ginger and pineapple

175g flour

1 teaspoon ground ginger

1 teaspoon ground white pepper

1 teaspoon ground four-spice

300g marzipan

300g sugar

200g honey

## Pineapple and Banana Semolina Cake

Preheat oven to 140°C. Grease and line the bottom of
a 24cm springform pan with greaseproof paper. Dust
bottom of pan with icing sugar to cover.

Remove skin from pineapple and slice into thin rounds.
Cut each round into 4 pieces and cut out the core. Arrange
in a circular pattern on base of pan, overlapping slightly.

Cream the butter and sugar in a mixer until light and fluffy.
Add eggs, one at a time. Add semolina, almond meal and
cinnamon and mix in. Sift in flour and baking powder.
Once flour is combined, fold through banana puree.

Place in pan and give a few taps to settle the mix. Bake for
1½ hours or until rich brown and well risen. Remove pan
from oven and transfer to a wire rack to cool before turning
out upside down.

Serve with cream or yoghurt.

I don't eat a lot of cake, but a previous pastry chef
of mine, Emma Mackay, cooks a wonderful fig and
semolina cake that I always remember. I think this
version is equally delicious. Jeremy.

**To serve eight people**

icing sugar
1 small pineapple
200g butter
320g caster sugar
6 free-range eggs
100g semolina
100g almond meal
1 teaspoon cinnamon
200g plain flour
1 teaspoon baking powder
180g banana puree

## Strawberry and Rhubarb Loaf

Preheat oven to 160°C. Grease a 22 x 12 x 6cm loaf pan with soft butter or oil. Dust with flour and tap out any excess.

In a mixer beat butter and caster sugar until light and fluffy. Add eggs, one at a time, then yoghurt and mix until combined. Fold through dry ingredients (reserving raw sugar) and, when fully mixed, fold through strawberries and rhubarb.

Place batter in loaf pan and spread evenly with a spatula. Sprinkle evenly with raw sugar. Bake in oven for 1 hour or until a skewer inserted into the centre comes out clean.

Transfer pan to a rack to cool for 10 minutes. Turn out and allow to finish cooling on rack. Slice and serve.

This loaf can be eaten toasted for breakfast, with coffee for afternoon tea, or as a simple dessert with chopped strawberries and yoghurt or whipped cream. Jane.

**To serve eight people**

110g unsalted butter, softened

200g caster sugar

3 free-range eggs

180g natural yoghurt

250g plain flour

1 pinch sea salt

8 medium strawberries, cut into
  quarters, washed

3 sticks rhubarb, cut into
  ½cm slices, washed

2 teaspoons baking powder

2 tablespoons raw sugar

# School nights.

Cooking on a school night should be quick and easy but full of flavour. The recipes in this chapter are designed to be one-dish meals. They are easily multiplied if you're feeding more than two. You could also combine different dishes to create two- or three-course meals. For example, a soup or small salad can be followed by a fish, meat or pasta dish. And for those who have a sweet tooth, we've included a few luscious desserts.

## Cauliflower Soup with Parmesan Wafers

Melt butter in a heavy-based saucepan on medium-low heat. Add onions, season well and sweat until completely soft. Add cauliflower and sweat for 5 minutes.

Add stock and bring to the boil. Simmer until cauliflower is completely soft and starting to break down. Remove from heat, puree mixture with a hand blender or jug blender until smooth. Pass through a conical strainer.

To make the wafers, preheat oven to 170°C. Line a baking tray with greaseproof paper and sprinkle parmesan in 2 circle shapes. Bake until golden brown and crisp, then transfer to a paper towel.

Pour hot soup into 2 bowls and serve topped with wafers.

This is a twist on cauliflower cheese. The textural combination of the velvety soup and the crisp wafer is excellent. Jeremy.

**To serve two people**

50g unsalted butter
1 large brown onion, finely sliced
sea salt
freshly ground white pepper
350g cauliflower, roughly chopped
1L chicken stock or water
40g parmesan cheese, finely grated

## Celery Gazpacho with Tabasco Ice Cubes

To make Tabasco Ice Cubes, season tomato juice with
Tabasco to taste, pour into ice cube trays and freeze.

Blend all gazpacho ingredients with 320ml water until smooth,
pass through a conical strainer and season.

Pour soup into 2 bowls and add 2 or 3 ice cubes to each. Garnish
with a few celery leaves and a drizzle of olive oil and serve.

Gazpacho is a refreshing, clean soup that's perfect
as a starter in hot weather. The spice and acid really
get your tastebuds going. Celery is an underrated
vegetable, in my view, and lends itself well as a tomato
substitute in this recipe. The colour is beautiful and it
makes a great canapé when served in shot glasses at
cocktail parties. Jane.

**To serve two people**

600g celery, washed
   and roughly chopped

50g brown onion, roughly chopped

220g green capsicums, seeds
   removed, roughly chopped

200g cucumber, seeds removed,
   roughly chopped

220ml olive oil

220ml extra-virgin olive oil

60ml white-wine vinegar

2 slices  white bread

sea salt

freshly ground white pepper

celery leaves, to garnish

**Tabasco Ice Cubes**

100ml tomato juice

Tabasco sauce

## Celeriac Soup with Worcestershire Sauce

Melt butter in a heavy-based saucepan over low heat. Add onion, leek and celery and sweat until soft. Add celeriac and sweat for 5 minutes. Add 1L water, season and bring to the boil.

Add potato and simmer for 20 minutes or until potato is soft. Remove from heat, blend until smooth and pass through a conical strainer.

Season to taste and pour into 2 soup bowls. Add a dash or two of Worcestershire sauce and a drizzle of cream and serve.

Many of my soups are made with water – it keeps them vegetarian and achieves a nice clean flavour. It also seems pointless to me to make vegetable stock for soups of this sort. This is based on the classic leek and potato soup and is one I rush to make as soon as the first celeriacs arrive in autumn. Jeremy.

**To serve two people**

60g unsalted butter

½ small brown onion, diced into 1cm pieces

¼ leek, washed, diced into 1cm pieces

1 celery stick, washed, diced into 1cm pieces

1 small celeriac, peeled, diced into 1cm pieces

sea salt

freshly ground white pepper

1 medium potato, peeled, diced into 1cm pieces

Worcestershire sauce

1 tablespoon cream (35% fat content)

## Chilled Pea Soup with Minted Crème Fraiche

Melt butter in a saucepan over medium-low heat. Add onion, season and sweat until soft. Add stock or water and bring to the boil. Add peas and cook, stirring, until the liquid just starts to simmer but has not re-boiled. Remove from heat and blend in a jug blender or with a stick blender until as smooth as possible. Pass through a conical strainer and check seasoning. Chill in the fridge.

Stir mint through crème fraiche. Pour soup into 2 bowls, dollop on crème fraiche and serve.

The trick with this soup is not to overcook the peas. This way you will maintain that brilliant green pea colour. This soup is just as good heated up – just be careful not to re-boil. Serve with crusty bread and you can garnish with thin, crispy bacon. Jane.

**To serve two people**

50g unsalted butter

1 medium brown onion, finely chopped

sea salt

freshly ground white pepper

1L chicken stock or water

600g frozen peas

1 sprig mint, leaves picked and finely sliced

2 tablespoons crème fraiche

## Spicy Sweet Potato and Red Lentil Soup

Heat a little olive oil in a heavy-based saucepan on medium-low heat. Add onion, ginger, chilli and garlic and season well. Sweat until soft and then add curry powder, mustard seeds, cardamom and bay leaf. Cook for a further 5 minutes to refresh spices.

Add sweet potato, tomatoes, lentils and stock or water. Bring to the boil, then reduce heat and simmer for 30 minutes or until lentils and sweet potato are soft.

Add peas and spinach and cook for 3 minutes or until peas are ready.

Season to taste and serve in 2 soup bowls with a dollop of yoghurt and a garnish of coriander.

This soup is truly a meal in a bowl. It is nutritious, filling and hearty. By reducing the liquid to 400ml you can make it less like a soup and more like a stew. Serve the stew with roasted fish, chicken or good-quality sausages. Jane.

**To serve two people**

olive oil

1 medium brown onion, finely sliced

1 knob ginger, finely chopped

1 small red chilli, finely chopped

2 garlic cloves, finely chopped

sea salt

freshly ground white pepper

1 tablespoon curry powder

1 tablespoon mustard seeds

4 cardamom pods

1 bay leaf

1 medium sweet potato, washed, diced into 1cm pieces

4 roma tomatoes, diced

¼ cup red lentils, washed

600ml chicken stock or water

60g peas

50g baby spinach

natural yoghurt, to serve

½ bunch coriander, leaves picked and roughly chopped, to garnish

# Green Lentil and Smoked Ham Hock Soup

To make the stock, place all stock ingredients in a saucepan, cover with cold water and bring to the boil. Simmer gently for 2–2½ hours or until meat falls away from the bone.

Remove hock from liquid and pass liquid through a fine strainer. Reserve 100ml of stock.

Remove ham from the bone, discarding skin, fat, gristle and bone. Leave meat in chunks and set aside in a little of the stock to keep moist. (Refrigerated, the stock will jelly and keep for at least a week.)

To make the soup, melt the butter over medium-low heat in a heavy-based saucepan. Add onion, leek and celery and sweat for 15 minutes or until soft. Add lentils and stock and bring to the boil. Season, reduce heat and simmer for 30 minutes or until lentils are very soft.

Remove from heat, blend until smooth and pass through a conical strainer. Season to taste, pour into 2 soup bowls and garnish with a few chunks of ham and chopped parsley.

This idea came from the classic pea and ham soup. I love its richness and the use of the hock stock ensures a lot of flavour. Try and find Puy lentils from France or Australian tiny dark green lentils, as they have a superior flavour and texture compared with the larger, paler green lentils. This soup keeps well in the fridge for up to 5 days. Jeremy.

**To serve two people**

40g unsalted butter

1 small brown onion, diced into 1cm pieces

¼ leek, washed, diced into 1cm pieces

1 celery stick, washed, diced into 1cm pieces

150g green or Puy lentils

sea salt

freshly ground white pepper

2 sprigs flat-leaf parsley, leaves picked and chopped, to garnish

**Smoked ham hock stock**

1 small smoked ham hock

1 small carrot, peeled

1 small brown onion, halved

1 stick celery, halved

1 bay leaf

2 sprigs thyme

1 teaspoon black peppercorns

*Note: Puy lentils are small green lentils from the French region of Puy. In Australia they are now called Australian French-style lentils, because of regional recognition laws. They are available at specialty food shops.*

## Minestrone of Summer Vegetables
## with Roasted Garlic Mayonnaise

To make Roasted Garlic Mayonnaise, preheat oven to 150°C. Drizzle unpeeled garlic with a little olive oil, wrap in aluminium foil and roast for 40 minutes or until very soft. Remove from foil and push through a fine sieve. Mix thoroughly into the mayonnaise. Season and leave at room temperature.

Warm 100ml of olive oil in a heavy-based saucepan over medium-low heat. Add sliced garlic, onion, leek and celery and sweat for 10 minutes or until half cooked. Add tomato paste and cook for 5 minutes, stirring regularly.

Add stock, bay leaf and thyme and bring to the boil. Season, reduce heat and simmer for 20 minutes.

Meanwhile, bring the cannellini beans to the boil in a saucepan of water. Reduce heat and simmer for 30 minutes or until soft, then drain. Remove bay leaf and thyme.

Add beans to the soup with the remaining vegetables, reheat and pour into soup bowls.

Garnish with basil and a dollop of mayonnaise. Serve with grilled sourdough.

I've served many versions of minestrone over the years. This is the basic recipe, to which you can add yabbies (a favourite of mine) or flaked salt cod. During cooking, you can add a slice of parmesan rind for extra flavour – remove it after the soup is cooked. Jeremy.

**To serve two people**

100ml olive oil

2 garlic cloves, thinly sliced

1 large brown onion, diced into 1cm pieces

1 small leek, washed, diced into 1cm pieces

1 celery stick, washed, diced into 1cm pieces

1 tablespoon tomato paste

1L chicken stock

1 bay leaf

1 sprig thyme

½ cup cannellini beans, soaked in cold water overnight

4 baby carrots, peeled, thinly sliced, blanched

10 green beans, blanched, diced into 1cm pieces

½ cup peas, blanched

¼ cup broad beans, blanched, peeled

6 snow peas, cut into small diamonds, blanched

4 leaves basil, torn, to garnish

**Roasted Garlic Mayonnaise**

½ head garlic, unpeeled

olive oil

4 tablespoons mayonnaise

sea salt

freshly ground white pepper

## Smoked Kingfish, Celery, Avocado and Rocket Salad

Cut avocado in half and remove seed. Scoop out cheeks and slice into four. Place in a large bowl and toss together with all the other ingredients. Season and dress with lemon juice and olive oil.

Pile salad evenly on 2 plates. Serve with crusty brown bread.

This is my favourite salad. I could eat it almost every day. The flavours are strong and clean, and the kingfish and avocado voluptuous. Smoked kingfish is a wonderful product; you may have to go to the fish markets to find it. If you are unable to, then substitute it with smoked trout, which is readily available. Jane.

**To serve two people**

1 ripe avocado

200g smoked kingfish or trout, skinned, boned, flaked

1 stick celery, washed, finely sliced diagonally

1 pinch pale celery leaves, washed

1 small handful baby rocket, washed, stems discarded

5 sprigs dill, leaves picked and washed

sea salt

freshly ground white pepper

1 tablespoon lemon juice

5 tablespoons olive oil

## Bread, Olive, Prosciutto and Balsamic Salad

Sprinkle eggplant with table salt and allow to stand for half an hour. Wash and pat dry with paper towel.

Shallow-fry eggplant in olive oil until golden brown. Drain on paper towel and set aside to cool.

Place bread, olives, prosciutto, parsley and eggplant in a large bowl and mix with Onion Dressing.

Season and serve in 2 bowls.

Bread salads have always intrigued me, so I have really enjoyed experimenting with them on the menu. The bread helps to make the salad more of a meal and adds plenty of texture and flavour. This salad is packed with intensely flavoured ingredients and could handle a few salad leaves if you want to lighten it. Gordal olives are large Spanish green olives available from specialty food stores. Normal green olives are a reasonable substitute. Jane.

**To serve two people**

½ small eggplant, diced into 1cm pieces

table salt

olive oil

2 slices sourdough bread, torn, oven-toasted until golden

6 Gordal olives, flesh cut from seeds

6 thin slices prosciutto

6 sprigs flat-leaf parsley, leaves picked and washed

Onion Dressing (see recipe page 16)

sea salt

freshly ground white pepper

## Baby Spinach, Tomato and Marinated Goat's Cheese Salad

To make Basic Salad Dressing, blend all ingredients together in a bowl with a whisk or stick blender until emulsified. Season to taste and store in a jar or a squeeze bottle. (This will make approximately 500ml. It will keep in the fridge for up to 3 months.)

Mix all salad ingredients in a bowl. Shake dressing to emulsify. Dress and season salad and serve on 2 plates.

A lovely, fresh, very simple and very quick recipe. Here I have given you Jane's recipe for a basic salad dressing – it's the best I've come across. Jeremy.

### To serve two people

5 cubes marinated fresh
   goat's cheese
4 roma tomatoes, each cut into
   8 wedges
1 large handful baby spinach,
   leaves picked and washed
12 thin slices baguette, toasted
12 kalamata olives, pitted
sea salt
freshly ground white pepper

### Basic Salad Dressing

125ml olive oil
200ml extra-virgin olive oil
80ml sherry vinegar
25ml good-quality red-wine vinegar
1 teaspoon Dijon mustard
2 tablespoon sugar
1 teaspoon salt
freshly ground white pepper

## Three–Tomato Salad with Avocado Mayonnaise

Preheat oven to 180°C. Lay roma tomatoes on a tray and sprinkle with sugar, salt and pepper. Drizzle with olive oil and balsamic vinegar. Bake for 20 minutes, then set aside.

To make Avocado Mayonnaise, mash avocado with a fork, add lemon juice and mayonnaise and season.

Arrange roma tomatoes evenly on 2 plates. Combine cherry tomatoes and semi-dried tomatoes in a bowl, then pile on top of the romas.

Dollop Avocado Mayonnaise in the middle of the salad and sprinkle with chives.

Make this salad in summer when the tomatoes are at their peak. It can be eaten on its own or as an accompaniment to other salads, cold meats or barbecues. Jane.

**To serve two people**

3 roma tomatoes, halved lengthways
sugar
sea salt
freshly ground white pepper
olive oil
balsamic vinegar
10 cherry tomatoes, halved
10 semi-dried tomatoes
½ bunch chives, cut into 3cm lengths

**Avocado Mayonnaise**
½ avocado
1 teaspoon lemon juice
2 tablespoons mayonnaise

## Calamari, Chorizo Sausage, Labna and Cucumber Salad

To make labna, stir together yoghurt and oil and drain through a coffee filter for at least 2 days (and up to 1 week) in the fridge. Remove from filter, roll into balls and store in a clean container. If storing for long periods, cover with vegetable oil.

Heat a non-stick frying pan over medium heat. Add a little olive oil and fry sausage slices until crispy on both sides. Remove and keep warm in a bowl.

Season calamari and gently fry in same pan for 3 minutes. Transfer to bowl with sausage.

Place a tablespoon of labna in the centre of 2 bowls. Sprinkle over cucumber. Top with warm calamari and sausage.

Dress rocket with Basic Salad Dressing and pile on top of calamari to serve.

My first taste of labna – dried yoghurt often used in Middle Eastern dishes – was in Melbourne. I fell in love with it straightaway. It's rich, smooth and sharp all at the same time. I did a little research and found that it is very easy to make yourself. I use it in loads of salads and it's especially good with Mediterranean flavours and beetroot. Jane.

**To serve two people**

olive oil

150g chorizo sausage, thinly sliced

sea salt

freshly ground white pepper

2 x 150g calamari, body and tentacles trimmed, cleaned, cut into strips

½ continental cucumber, cut in half lengthways, seeds removed, thinly sliced

1 small handful young rocket

Basic Salad Dressing (see recipe on page 54)

**Labna**

200g natural yoghurt

50ml olive oil

## Mussel, Leek and Saffron Mayonnaise Salad

To cook the mussels, heat a little olive oil in a large saucepan over high heat. When hot, add onion, celery, leek, garlic, peppercorns, bay leaf and thyme and cook for 3 minutes. Add white wine and bring to the boil.

Add mussels and cook, stirring. As soon as the mussels open, pick them out with tongs and place in a bowl so they won't overcook.

Remove saucepan from heat and strain liquid. Pick mussels out of shell, checking for any remaining beards, and store in some of the strained liquid.

Heat a barbecue or open grill. Rub leeks and capsicum with olive oil and grill on both sides until just cooked.

Place saffron in a saucepan with 20ml water, bring to the boil, then remove from heat and stand for 10 minutes to infuse. Pass through a fine strainer into mayonnaise and mix well.

Place leek and capsicum on 2 plates. Surround with mussels, season and drizzle with some mayonnaise.

Toss salad leaves together with a small amount of mayonnaise, pile on top and serve.

Mussels and saffron have always been great together, whether in soups or sauces for fish. This salad makes a lovely light lunch. Jeremy.

### To serve two people

12 baby leeks, trimmed, washed

1 red capsicum, cut into 8, seeds removed

1 pinch saffron

4 tablespoons mayonnaise

sea salt

freshly ground white pepper

1 small handful young rocket, washed

6 sprigs chervil, leaves picked and washed

6 sprigs flat parsley, leaves picked and washed

6 sprigs watercress, leaves picked and washed

### Mussels
olive oil

½ brown onion, finely sliced

1 stick celery, washed, chopped

½ leek, chopped and washed

2 garlic cloves, crushed

1 teaspoon white peppercorns

1 bay leaf

2 sprigs thyme

250ml white wine

1kg black mussels, washed, de-bearded

## Roast Chicken, Mixed Bean and Champagne Vinegar Salad

Place cannellini beans in a saucepan and cover with cold water. Bring to the boil, skim any impurities from surface and then simmer for 20 minutes or until beans are soft. Drain and allow to cool.

Mix all ingredients in a bowl, season and dress with Champagne Vinegar Dressing.

Place in 2 bowls and serve with crusty bread.

The Champagne Vinegar Dressing and the fresh herbs are what takes this salad to the next level. Perfect for a picnic lunch. Jane.

### To serve two people

30g dried cannellini beans, soaked in water overnight

75g green beans, blanched, pulled in half lengthways

50g fresh borlotti beans, boiled in seasoned chicken stock or water until soft

½ roast chicken, meat shredded

¼ bunch flat parsley, leaves picked and washed

3 sprigs basil, leaves picked and torn

sea salt

freshly ground white pepper

### Champagne Vinegar Dressing

Follow the Onion Dressing recipe on page 16, using champagne vinegar in place of balsamic vinegar.

## Penne with Spicy Sausage and Tomato

Heat a little olive oil in a heavy-based saucepan over medium heat. Add onions and garlic, season well and cook for 15 minutes or until very soft. Add sausage and cook for 5 minutes. Add tomatoes and a pinch of sugar. Simmer on medium-low heat for 20 minutes, stirring and breaking up tomatoes slightly, or until sauce has thickened.

Meanwhile, cook pasta in a large pot of boiling salted water until al dente. Drain and toss lightly in olive oil.

Add peas and spinach to sauce, cook for 1 minute and season to taste. Stir pasta through sauce and divide between 2 large bowls.

Serve with parmesan, if desired, and a green salad.

We first made this pasta dish one night when there was hardly anything in the cupboard. We didn't even have the spinach – this was a later addition. It was so tasty that it's now a regular feature. Choose a spicy sausage with plenty of flavour, such as chorizo or a good salami. Jeremy.

**To serve two people**

50ml olive oil

2 medium Spanish onions, finely sliced

1 garlic clove, finely sliced

sea salt

freshly ground white pepper

100g spicy sausage, thinly sliced

1 x 400g can whole tomatoes

1 pinch white sugar

300g penne

80g peas

1 handful baby spinach

## Pan-fried Gnocchi with Pumpkin, Ricotta and Sage

Preheat oven to 180°C.

To make gnocchi, cook potatoes in their skins in boiling salted water until soft. Drain, peel and pass through a mouli (you will need 400g cooked potatoes).

Place potato on a bench and sprinkle over salt and flour. With a knife or pastry card, chop potatoes to incorporate flour without overworking. Once mixture starts to form dry lumps, use your hands to bring it together and knead gently into a ball. Keep kneading until mixture is smooth and not sticky – you may need to add flour to the bench as you go. Wrap in a tea towel and set aside to rest for 20 minutes.

Meanwhile, place pumpkin on a roasting tray, drizzle with olive oil and season. Bake in oven for 20 minutes or until golden brown and soft. Remove from oven, drain and set aside.

To finish gnocchi, cut into 4 pieces. Roll each piece into a 2cm-wide log and then cut into 2cm-long 'pillows'. Cook in a pot of boiling salted water until gnocchi floats to the surface. Refresh in iced water. When cold, drain, drizzle with oil to prevent sticking together, and set aside.

Heat a non-stick frying pan with a little vegetable oil over medium heat and fry gnocchi on both sides until golden brown. Add pumpkin and butter and fry until butter turns golden brown. Add sage and divide quickly between 2 large bowls.

Sprinkle with ricotta and serve.

I much prefer the texture of pan-fried gnocchi to boiled. The combination of sage and brown butter is an absolute classic and the feel of cold ricotta is wonderful with the other hot ingredients. If pushed for time, you could buy ready-made gnocchi from a good food store. Jeremy.

**To serve two people**

500g desiree potatoes, washed
1 tablespoon table salt
100g plain flour
300g butternut pumpkin, peeled, de-seeded, diced into 2cm pieces
olive oil
sea salt
freshly ground white pepper
vegetable oil
40g unsalted butter
8 sage leaves, finely shredded
50g ricotta

## Cauliflower, Blue Cheese and Baby Spinach Risoni

Melt butter in a saucepan over medium heat, add onion, season and cook until soft. Add cauliflower and cook for 2 minutes. Add risoni and stock or water and cook for 15 minutes or until risoni is al dente and liquid is absorbed (add more liquid if needed).

Stir through spinach and crumble over cheese. Cook for 2 minutes and season to taste.

Place in 2 bowls and serve.

Cauliflower and cheese are like peaches and cream – they are meant for each other. You can substitute the blue cheese with your favourite cheese, as long as it melts well. This is quite a rich meal. The spinach helps to cut the richness and it is perfect served with a crisp green salad. Jane.

**To serve two people**

50g unsalted butter

1 medium brown onion, finely sliced

sea salt

freshly ground white pepper

¼ cauliflower, cut into florets

160g risoni

500ml chicken or vegetable stock

50g baby spinach

50g blue cheese

## Spaghetti with Chilli, Garlic, White Wine and Tiny Clams

Place olive oil in a large heavy-based saucepan (that has a lid). Add garlic and place on high heat. As garlic begins to fry, stir to cook evenly, until light golden in colour. Add chilli and immediately add white wine. Keep on high heat and allow the wine to boil and reduce by half. The garlic will now be very soft and a deep golden brown.

Cook spaghetti in a large saucepan of boiling salted water until al dente. Drain and set aside.

Meanwhile, add clams to garlic base and cover saucepan with lid. Cook on medium heat for 2 minutes. Stir quickly, replace lid and cook for a further 2 minutes or until clams open. Add spaghetti and parsley, season to taste and place in 2 large bowls.

Serve with a green salad and crusty bread.

Whoever invented this dish should be given a medal. It is a classic for so many wonderful reasons. I particularly love opening the saucepan lid, being hit with all those heady aromas for the first time and anticipating the first mouthful. The important part of this method is when to add the chilli and wine. If you don't cook the garlic enough – to a light golden-brown colour – you won't achieve a deep enough flavour. And if you take it too far, the end result will be bitter. It's well worth the risk and the base can be used for lots of other things such as a baste for seafood. Jane.

**To serve two people**

200ml olive oil

3 garlic cloves, finely sliced

1 small red chilli, unseeded, finely sliced

150ml dry white wine

250g spaghetti

500g vongole clams, soaked in water for a few hours to remove grit

½ bunch flat-leaf parsley, picked, washed, roughly chopped

sea salt

freshly ground white pepper

## Smoked Salmon, Pea and Crème Fraiche Risotto

To make risotto base, bring stock to a simmer in a heavy-based saucepan. Melt the butter in another heavy-based saucepan over medium heat. Add onions, season well and sweat until soft. Add rice and cook for 3 minutes. Add stock, a large ladle at a time, stirring continuously. As liquid is absorbed, add more until rice is cooked to al dente. This should take about 10 minutes. Add more stock if necessary.

Add peas, smoked salmon and crème fraiche and stir through. Season to taste.

Divide between 2 bowls, sprinkle with dill and serve.

Peas and crème fraiche are a great combination. The smoked salmon adds plenty of flavour and the dill freshens the dish and cuts the richness. This would make a lovely entrée if kept small. Jane.

### To serve two people

60g peas, blanched

6 slices smoked salmon, finely sliced

2 tablespoons crème fraiche

2 sprigs dill, leaves picked and roughly chopped

### Risotto base

500ml chicken or vegetable stock

40g unsalted butter

1 medium brown onion, finely diced

sea salt

freshly ground white pepper

200g risotto rice

## Asparagus, Walnut and Lemon Thyme Risotto

Make risotto base as for recipe opposite.

Cut asparagus into 5 even lengths. When risotto is just cooked, stir in asparagus, parmesan, butter and thyme, season to taste and serve in 2 bowls.

Sprinkle with walnuts and serve.

This risotto is lovely when you use the first asparagus in spring. The unique dry texture of walnuts and the fragrance of lemon thyme make it a little different. The best way to trim asparagus is to snap off the ends, allowing it to break where it wants to. This will ensure that the woody end is discarded. Jane.

### To serve two people

1 bunch asparagus, peeled at stalk end, trimmed, blanched

40g parmesan, grated

10g butter, to garnish

6 sprigs lemon thyme, leaves picked

20g walnuts, lightly roasted, crushed

### Risotto base

500ml chicken or vegetable stock

40g unsalted butter

1 medium brown onion, finely diced

sea salt

freshly ground white pepper

200g risotto rice

## Mushroom and Thyme Risoni

Heat olive oil in a large heavy-based saucepan over medium heat. Add onion and garlic, season well, and cook until onion is completely soft and starting to colour slightly.

Add mushrooms, thyme and bay leaf and cook for 30 minutes or until mushrooms are soft and liquid is evaporated. Add risoni and stock or water and simmer, stirring, for 20 minutes or until risoni is just cooked and liquid is absorbed. Add more liquid if necessary.

Stir through parsley and pecorino and season to taste. Spoon into 2 bowls and serve with a green salad or steamed green vegetables dressed with olive oil.

The first time I cooked risoni I was staying with a friend in Western Australia. I was a bit dubious as to how it was going to work, but she assured me that it was similar to cooking risotto. The result was far better than I had anticipated and I now enjoy eating and cooking risoni more than risotto. It is easy to control the cooking and has fantastic mouthfeel. Stirring through peas or baby spinach at the end is a convenient way to get your green-vegetable fix and makes for a complete meal in a bowl. Jane.

**To serve two people**

150ml olive oil

2 medium Spanish onions, finely sliced

2 cloves garlic, chopped

sea salt

freshly ground white pepper

4 large field mushrooms, finely sliced

2 sprigs thyme

1 bay leaf

150g risoni

500ml chicken or vegetable stock

½ bunch flat-leaf parsley, leaves picked and finely shredded

50g pecorino

## Zucchini Flower, Saffron and Pecorino Risotto

To make the risotto base, bring stock to the boil, add saffron, remove from heat and allow to infuse for 10 minutes. Complete base by following recipe on page 67.

Add zucchini flowers to risotto base with stems, pecorino and butter.

Season to taste and serve in 2 bowls.

Chefs always get excited when summer delivers zucchini flowers, and Jane and I are no exception. There are so many uses for zucchini flowers and, in my 25 years of cooking, I can't remember a restaurant that hasn't had them on the menu. My fondest memories are stuffing them at Roger Vergé's restaurant in the south of France. Always use saffron pistils, never the powder. They are worth the extra cost as they have a far better flavour. Be careful not to overdo it with saffron, as it can easily overpower a dish. Jeremy.

**To serve two people**

6 female zucchini flowers, stamens and pistils removed, stems reserved, finely sliced, blanched

50g pecorino

10g unsalted butter

sea salt

freshly ground white pepper

**Risotto base**

500ml chicken or vegetable stock

1 pinch saffron

40g unsalted butter

1 medium brown onion, finely diced

200g risotto rice

## Blue Eye Wrapped in Prosciutto with
## Sweet Potato and Caramelised Witlof

Preheat oven to 160°C. Place witlof, a pinch of sugar and salt, lemon juice, 20g butter and 180ml water in a small baking dish and cover with greaseproof paper. Place in oven and cook for 40 minutes or until witlof is caramelised. Remove from dish, cut in half and set aside.

Cut sweet potato into two 4cm-long pieces and place in a small saucepan, flat-side down. Add 50g butter, season and just cover with water. Boil rapidly on high until potato is cooked and water evaporates. Potato will then fry in the remaining butter. Do not disturb potato and allow bottom of pan to go dark brown. Remove pan from heat and allow to settle for a few minutes before gently removing potato. The potato bottoms should be a deep golden colour. Set aside and keep warm.

Wrap each fish fillet in 2 prosciutto slices to cover. Heat a non-stick frying pan with a little vegetable oil over high heat. Cook fish on both sides and place in oven for 6–7 minutes or until just cooked.

Meanwhile, heat another non-stick frying pan and sprinkle in remaining sugar. Allow to caramelise to a deep brown colour. Add remaining butter to stop caramelisation and then add witlof, with inside facing down. Cook for 2–3 minutes, turn over and cook for a further 2 minutes.

Place witlof in centre of 2 plates, with inside facing up. Lay fish over witlof and place sweet potato, golden side up, on the side.

Serve with green salad or steamed green vegetables.

**To serve two people**

2 small witlof

40g caster sugar

sea salt

½ lemon, juiced

100g unsalted butter

1 small sweet potato

freshly ground white pepper

2 x 200g fillets blue eye,
    skinned, boned

4 thin prosciutto slices

vegetable oil

Jeremy and I are both fond of teaming meat with fish. The prosciutto adds great flavour to this dish and protects the fish while cooking, keeping it moist. As prosciutto is salty, I've used sweet potato to contrast and the witlof adds some sweetness as well as acid. The colours of this dish are all golden and inviting. It makes a great dinner-party dish, so just double or triple the quantities when catering for more. Jane.

## Snapper with Soft Polenta, Radicchio and Garlic

Preheat oven to 200°C.

Bring the milk and 250ml water to the boil in a heavy-based saucepan, pour in polenta in a steady stream and whisk vigorously until polenta starts to thicken. Reduce heat to low and cook gently for about 30 minutes, then add another 50ml water and cook for another 15 minutes, stirring regularly, or until polenta is smooth and no longer grainy.

Meanwhile, mix together radicchio, parsley, garlic and olive oil and set aside. Heat a non-stick ovenproof frying pan with a little vegetable oil over medium heat. Season snapper and fry, skin side down, for 2 minutes or until golden brown. Turn over and fry for another 2 minutes. Turn back on skin side and roast in oven for 5 minutes or until just cooked.

Transfer frying pan to cooktop, add prawns and cook each side on medium heat for 1 minute.

Divide polenta between 2 large soup plates. Top with snapper and then prawns.

Drain fish pan of cooking oil, return to a medium heat, add radicchio mix and fry until radicchio wilts. Season with plenty of salt, pepper and lemon juice. Spoon around snapper and serve.

Polenta is rich in texture but can be quite bland. It teams really well with other strong flavours such as lemon, parsley, garlic and salt, so make sure to season your radicchio well to make this dish really work. Jane.

**To serve two people**

500ml milk

120g white polenta

1 small radicchio, washed, finely sliced

8 sprigs flat-leaf parsley, washed, leaves picked and finely shredded

2 garlic cloves, finely chopped

100ml olive oil

vegetable oil

sea salt

freshly ground cracked pepper

2 x 200g fillets snapper, skin on, boned

4 medium green prawns, peeled, intestines removed

1 lemon, juiced

*Note: White polenta is 100% maize flour and can be found at specialty food stores. You can substitute it with the more common yellow polenta or cornmeal, as long as it is 100%, with no additive flour.*

# Flathead with Mushrooms, Garlic, Parsley and Brown Butter

Heat a non-stick frying pan over medium heat. Add 40g butter and, once hot, add mushrooms and garlic. Season and fry on medium heat until golden brown.

In a separate non-stick frying pan, heat remaining butter over medium heat. Season fish, add to pan and cook on each side for 3 minutes or until just cooked and golden brown.

Add parsley to mushrooms and season to taste. Spoon onto 2 plates and top with fish.

Serve with creamy mashed potato and steamed green vegetables.

Few can resist mushrooms and garlic cooked in butter, especially with plenty of parsley tossed in at the end to freshen it. I especially enjoy them on a slice of sourdough toast for breakfast. Flathead is a fine flaked white fish with enough flavour of its own to pair well with the full-flavoured mushrooms. Other white fish such as snapper or blue eye will do. Jane.

**To serve two people**

60g unsalted butter

75g Swiss brown mushrooms, stalks removed, finely sliced

75g oyster mushrooms, stalks removed, torn into 1cm pieces

75g enoki mushrooms, stalks trimmed

1 garlic clove, finely chopped

sea salt

freshly ground white pepper

2 x 200g fillets flathead, skinned, boned

8 sprigs flat-leaf parsley, washed, leaves picked and roughly chopped

## Roast Barramundi with White Bean Stew

Preheat oven to 200°C. Reheat White Bean Stew.

Meanwhile, heat a non-stick frying pan with a little vegetable oil over medium heat. Fry barramundi, skin side down, for 2 minutes or until golden brown. Turn over and fry a further 2 minutes. Turn back on skin side, place pan in oven and roast for 5 minutes or until just cooked. Remove fish and keep warm.

Wipe out frying pan with paper towel. Return to medium heat and add butter. When butter starts to froth, add spinach, season and cook until it just wilts. Remove from pan and drain on paper towel.

Divide White Bean Stew between 2 large soup plates. Top with barramundi, then spinach, and serve.

While working for Pierre Koffmann in London, I was inspired by his combinations of fish and meat. The richness of this stew cooked with bacon goes beautifully with a roasted piece of fish. I prefer wild barramundi to farmed, as the flavour of farmed can be quite 'muddy'. Other white fish such as snapper or blue eye make fine alternatives. Jeremy.

**To serve two people**

2 serves White Bean Stew
  (see recipe on page 14)
vegetable oil
2 x 200g fillets barramundi,
  skin on, boned
15g unsalted butter
100g baby spinach
sea salt
freshly ground white pepper

## Rainbow Trout with Fennel and Star Anise Puree and Baby Spinach

Melt 40g butter in a heavy-based medium-sized saucepan over medium heat. Add onion, season well and sweat until soft. Add fennel and star anise, just cover with water and simmer for 30 minutes or until fennel is very soft and starting to break down. Remove star anise and, with a jug blender or hand blender, puree fennel mixture until very smooth. Pass through a conical strainer.

Heat a non-stick frying pan with a little vegetable oil over medium heat. Cook trout, skin side down, for 3 minutes or until golden brown. Turn over and cook for a further 1 minute. Remove from pan and keep warm.

Wipe out pan with paper towel and return to medium heat. Add remaining butter and, when foaming, add spinach, season and cook gently for 1 minute or until spinach wilts. Drain on paper towel.

Spoon fennel puree evenly on to the centre of 2 dinner plates. Top with trout fillets and then a pile of spinach. Drizzle plate with extra-virgin olive oil.

Farmed rainbow trout is readily available and inexpensive. Be sure to remove all the bones. Jeremy.

**To serve two people**

55g unsalted butter

1 small onion, finely sliced

sea salt

freshly ground white pepper

2 small fennel bulbs, shredded

1 star anise

vegetable oil

2 x 160g fillets rainbow trout, skin on, boned

100g baby spinach

extra-virgin olive oil

## Kingfish with a Pissaladière of White Anchovies and Green Olives

Melt butter and sugar in a heavy-based saucepan over low heat. Add onions, season and cook for 45 minutes, stirring regularly, until onions are very soft and golden brown.

Preheat oven to 180°C. Cut two 9cm-diameter circles from puff pastry and prick evenly with a fork. Lightly grease a baking tray, place pastry on tray and cover with a cooling rack to prevent it rising too much. Bake in oven for 15 minutes or until golden brown.

Heat a non-stick frying pan with a little vegetable oil over medium heat. Season kingfish and fry for 1–2 minutes each side or until golden brown. Place in oven and cook for 3–4 minutes, leaving fish slightly undercooked in the centre.

Meanwhile, spread a thin layer of onions over cooked pastry. (Any leftover onion can be refrigerated for up to a week.) Place anchovies in a noughts-and-crosses design over onions. Place an olive cheek in each space.

Warm olive oil in a saucepan over low heat, add salt, pepper, lemon juice and thyme. Make a small salad with the herbs and rocket and place at the top of 2 dinner plates. Place the tartlets below the salad and the fish on top.

Spoon warm dressing over fish and salad and serve.

Farmed kingfish has been a revelation in aquaculture recently. The tart is a play of a classic pissaladière. Gordal olives are large green Spanish olives with a superior flavour, but normal green olives could be used instead. The marinated white anchovies are a lot more subtle than their brown cousins but can be difficult to find, so use the best-quality anchovies available. Jeremy.

### To serve two people

40g unsalted butter

1 teaspoon caster sugar

2 medium brown onions, finely sliced

sea salt

freshly ground black pepper

1 layer good-quality puff pastry

vegetable oil

2 x 200g fillets kingfish, skinned

8 marinated white anchovies, halved lengthways

9 Gordal olives, cheeks sliced from seed

50ml extra-virgin olive oil

½ lemon, juiced

2 sprigs lemon thyme, leaves picked

1 sprig dill, leaves picked

2 sprigs flat-leaf parsley, picked

½ bunch chives, cut into 2cm pieces

20g rocket, washed, drained

## Poached Sand Whiting, Clams and Tagliatelle

Heat a little vegetable oil in a heavy-based saucepan over medium heat. Add eschalots, celery, bay leaf and thyme and fry for 1 minute. Add clams and wine and cover with a lid. Cook for 5 minutes or until clams open.

Transfer clams to a bowl with a slotted spoon. Pass cooking liquor through a fine strainer into a clean saucepan. Discard eschalots, celery and herbs. Cook liquid until reduced by half. Meanwhile, pick clams out of their shells and set aside.

Cook pasta in a saucepan of boiling salted water for 7 minutes or until al dente. While pasta is cooking, bring clam stock to a gentle simmer. Add whiting fillets and poach gently for 5 minutes or until just cooked.

Drain pasta and toss with 10g butter. Place pasta in 2 large bowls and lay whiting fillets alongside. Boil cooking liquor again and add cream. Bring back to the boil and whisk in remaining butter.

Add clams and chives, season to taste, pour over fish and serve.

During my 10 years in Melbourne I only ever cooked King George whiting. After arriving in Sydney I soon discovered sand whiting. It's slightly cheaper, with a firmer texture and slightly stronger flavour. Mussels can be substituted for clams, or use both. The liquor used to cook the shellfish is also used to poach the whiting, giving this dish its intensity. Jeremy.

**To serve two people**

vegetable oil

5 eschalots, finely sliced

1 stick celery, finely chopped

1 bay leaf

2 sprigs thyme

300g vongole clams, soaked in water to remove grit

300ml white wine

200g homemade or good-quality tagliatelle

4 x 100g fillets sand whiting, skin on, boned

40g unsalted butter

40ml cream (35% fat content)

1 bunch chives, finely chopped

sea salt

freshly ground white pepper

## Roast Salmon with Crushed Kipflers, Olives and Spring Onions

Preheat oven to 200°C.

Heat olive oil in a saucepan over low heat, add spring onions and sweat for 5 minutes. Add potatoes, season and crush with a fork – do not mash. Add olives and heat gently on low heat for 5 minutes, stirring constantly. Remove pan from heat and keep warm.

Heat a non-stick frying pan with a little vegetable oil over medium heat. Season salmon and fry, skin side down, for 2 minutes or until golden brown. Turn over and cook for a further 2 minutes. Turn back onto skin side and roast in oven for 4 minutes or until just cooked but still pink in the centre. Remove salmon from pan and keep warm.

Place tomatoes in the same pan, put in oven and roast for 2 minutes.

Place potatoes in the centre of 2 dinner plates, top with salmon, skin side up, and place tomatoes on one side. Drizzle with extra-virgin olive oil, sprinkle salmon skin with sea salt and serve.

Crushing potatoes (you can use any waxy potato) makes a rustic alternative to potato puree. We often serve ocean trout this way, instead of salmon. Jeremy.

**To serve two people**

1 tablespoon olive oil

3 spring onions, green part only, finely sliced

4 medium kipfler potatoes, washed, boiled in skin, peeled

sea salt

freshly ground white pepper

12 kalamata olives, pitted, roughly chopped

vegetable oil

2 x 200g fillets salmon, skin on, boned

2 bunches (about 10) cherry tomatoes on the vine

extra-virgin olive oil

## Spicy Seafood Stew with New Potatoes and Tomato

To make the stew base, heat olive oil in a heavy-based saucepan over medium-low heat. Add onion, ginger and garlic, season and cook until very soft. Add dry spices, thyme and bay leaf and cook for 5 minutes. Add tomatoes and chilli and simmer for 30 minutes or until sauce thickens. Season to taste.

Add seafood and potatoes and simmer gently until mussel shells open.

Divide stew between 2 bowls and garnish with coriander.

This stew is wonderfully aromatic and very healthy. If you make the base a few days in advance, then this dish can be on the table in minutes. The spices get better and better after a few days in the fridge so it's not a bad idea to do it this way. You could also make a large batch and keep some in the freezer if you're feeling super-organised. Jane.

**To serve two people**

250g fillet blue eye, skinned, cut
  into 6 cubes

150g calamari tube, halved
  lengthways, cleaned, cut into
  1cm strips

12 mussels, washed, beards removed

4 small pink-eye or kipfler potatoes,
  boiled, peeled, quartered

6 sprigs coriander, leaves picked
  and washed

**Stew base**

1 tablespoon olive oil

1 large brown onion, finely sliced

1 knob ginger, finely chopped

1 garlic clove, finely chopped

sea salt

freshly ground white pepper

½ teaspoon yellow mustard seeds

½ teaspoon ground coriander

3 cardamom pods

½ teaspoon ground turmeric

1 sprig thyme

1 bay leaf

400g crushed canned tomatoes

1 red chilli, finely chopped

## Fish Pie

Preheat oven to 200°C.

Cook potatoes in boiling salted water for 30 minutes or until soft. Drain, crush with a fork and reserve.

In a heavy-based saucepan melt butter over low heat and add onions. Season well and sweat until soft. Add flour and cook gently for 10 minutes, stirring constantly, to allow gluten in flour to cook. Add mustard and slowly add milk, stirring constantly so that no lumps develop. Bring to the boil, reduce heat to low and cook for a further 5 minutes, stirring, or until sauce thickens. Add fish and cook for 5 minutes, stirring occasionally.

Spoon into 2 medium-sized ceramic ramekins. Sprinkle evenly with peas. Top with potato and scatter over a few small knobs of butter. Bake in oven for 30 minutes or until potatoes start to colour.

Serve with green salad.

I first started making Fish Pie for staff meals at the restaurant as there is often plenty of good fish trim to use up. Everyone loves it and it's become a bit of a cult classic as far as staff meals go. Fish Pie is true comfort food - my mum has made a tuna version for as long as I can remember and it still hits the spot every time. Jane.

**To serve two people**

300g pontiac potatoes, peeled, quartered

40g unsalted butter, plus extra to garnish

1 medium brown onion, finely chopped

sea salt

freshly ground white pepper

2 tablespoons plain flour

1 tablespoon Dijon mustard

300ml milk

300g white fish, skinned, diced into 1½cm pieces

100g peas

## Free-range Chicken Breast
## with Red Rice and Hazelnuts

Preheat oven to 180°C.

Melt 30g butter in a small saucepan over low heat. Add onions and sweat until soft. Season mildly.

Drain rice and add to onions with 290ml stock. Bring to the boil. Add bay leaf and marjoram, cover with foil and a lid, place in oven and cook for 1 hour.

Heat a non-stick frying pan with a little vegetable oil over medium heat. Season chicken and place in pan, skin side down. Cook for 2 minutes or until skin starts to turn golden. Turn over and cook for a further 2 minutes. Turn again, add remaining butter, cover with foil to protect flesh from drying out and place in oven. Cook for 8–9 minutes, then remove chicken from pan and sit in a warm place.

Return pan to the heat and add remaining chicken stock. Simmer for 1 minute to make a sauce.

Remove rice from oven, discard marjoram and bay leaf, stir well and season to taste. Spoon rice into 2 large soup plates and top with chicken. Pour over sauce and sprinkle with hazelnuts.

Serve with steamed green beans.

Red rice comes from France and Indonesia. I prefer the French variety. It's a step up from brown rice, has a beautiful nutty flavour and plenty of fibre. It needs a long time to cook, so soaking overnight is essential. Cooking by absorption, as in this recipe, retains all the flavour and goodness. Hazelnuts enhance the rice's nutty flavour and are perfect with chicken. Red rice is available at specialty food stores. A good substitute is brown rice, which doesn't require soaking overnight. Jane.

**To serve two people**

50g unsalted butter

½ medium brown onion, finely chopped

sea salt

freshly ground white pepper

100g red rice, soaked in water overnight

340ml chicken stock

1 bay leaf

2 sprigs marjoram

vegetable oil

2 free-range chicken breasts, skin on

50g hazelnuts, roasted, peeled, roughly crushed

## Lamb Rump with Jerusalem Artichoke Puree and Pomegranate and Saba Sauce

Preheat oven to 200°C.

Heat butter in a small saucepan over medium-low heat. Add onions, season and sweat until soft.

Add artichokes and chicken stock or water and simmer, stirring occasionally to prevent sticking to the pan, until artichokes are very soft. Remove from heat. Using a blender, puree until completely smooth. Season to taste and keep warm.

Place pomegranate seeds and saba in a saucepan and simmer over very low heat for 10 minutes.

Meanwhile, heat a non-stick ovenproof frying pan with a little vegetable oil over high heat. Season lamb and fry for 1 minute on all sides to seal. Place fat-covered side down and place in oven. Roast for 7 minutes, then turn over and roast for a further 4–5 minutes. Transfer to a warm place to rest for 15 minutes.

Spoon artichoke puree on to the centre of 2 large plates. Cut each rump across the grain into six slices and place on top of puree. Season and drizzle with Pomegranate and Saba Sauce.

Rump is my favourite part of the lamb to cook. It's the perfect size for one serve and roasts well. As lamb is quite fatty, it's best served with something that cuts through the fat, such as the traditional mint sauce or jelly. Pomegranate and Saba Sauce does the same job. Saba is concentrated, reduced grape juice with a superb caramel flavour and can be bought at specialty food stores. If you can't find it, substitute with balsamic vinegar. Jane.

**To serve two people**

15g unsalted butter

½ small brown onion, finely sliced

sea salt

freshly ground white pepper

200g Jerusalem artichokes, peeled, sliced

200ml chicken stock or water

1 pomegranate, seeds removed

4 tablespoons saba

vegetable oil

2 x 180g lamb rumps, fat left on

## Marinated Spare Ribs

Mix all ingredients together in a large bowl. Add spare ribs and marinate for 1 hour.

Preheat a barbecue on high or an oven to 200°C. Remove spare ribs from marinade and grill for 10 minutes each side, or roast for 20 minutes.

Cut ribs between bones and serve with roast potatoes and a green salad.

This marinade is perfect for anything barbecued or roasted, such as chicken wings, other varieties of spare ribs and grilled meats. It has so much flavour that you shouldn't marinate anything in it for longer than 2 hours, and you can use the marinade again. It keeps for up to 4 days in the fridge. The spare ribs are best eaten with your hands. Jane.

**To serve two people**

125ml soy sauce

125ml white-wine vinegar

125ml tomato sauce or Tomato Jam
  (see recipe on page 10)

75g brown sugar

75g honey

1 tablespoon seeded mustard

2 garlic cloves, finely diced

1 knob ginger, peeled, finely diced

2 small red chillis, finely chopped

2kg American-style beef spare ribs

## Pan-fried Calf's Liver with Potato Puree, Braised Lettuce and Onion Gravy

To make Onion Gravy, melt the butter and sugar in a heavy-based saucepan over low heat. Add onion, season and cook, stirring regularly, for 45 minutes or until onion is very soft and golden brown. Add vinegar and reduce by three-quarters. Add wine and reduce to a syrup. Add veal stock and bring to the boil, then simmer until gravy is slightly thick. Skim any impurities from the surface. Season to taste and set aside.

Preheat oven to 180°C. Boil the chicken stock, then pour in a baking dish. Season, add lettuce, cover with foil and place in oven. Braise lettuce for 30 minutes or until core is tender. Remove from oven and keep warm.

To make Potato Puree, bring potatoes to the boil in salted water, then simmer until just cooked. Drain and pass through a mouli into a bowl. Place the milk, cream and butter in a saucepan, bring to the boil, then pour gradually over potatoes, stirring constantly until smooth. Season, cover and keep warm.

Heat a frying pan with a little vegetable oil over high heat. Season liver and sear on both sides for 30 seconds. Remove from pan, drain oil, add onion gravy and liver to pan. Bring back to the boil and cook for 2 minutes for medium, or longer if desired. Remove from heat.

Drain lettuce and cut in half. Place potato puree to the side of 2 dinner plates. Top with liver slices and place lettuce alongside. Pour over Onion Gravy and serve.

Liver may not be everyone's cup of tea, but I adore it. Potato puree and onion gravy always seem to be the natural accompaniments. The sharpness of the vinegar cuts the richness of the liver. The lettuce can be replaced with roast beetroot, and grilled bacon is another great addition. Cleaned and sliced liver is available from good butchers. Jeremy.

### To serve two people

1L chicken stock

1 medium cos lettuce, kept whole, washed, outer leaves discarded

vegetable oil

4 x 1cm-thick slices calf's liver

### Potato Puree

2 medium desiree potatoes, peeled, quartered

50ml milk

50ml cream (35% fat content)

25g unsalted butter

### Onion Gravy

30g unsalted butter

1 teaspoon caster sugar

1 medium brown onion, finely sliced

sea salt

freshly ground white pepper

2 teaspoons red-wine vinegar

30ml red wine

150ml veal stock

## Mixed Grill with Tomato Jam and Green Beans

Place butter, garlic and parsley in a bowl, season and mix well.
Lay a 25cm square piece of foil on a bench. Spoon butter mixture
onto centre and fold over foil. Roll into a log shape and twist ends.
Refrigerate until set. Cut four ½cm-thick slices, remove foil
and reserve.

Preheat an open grill or barbecue on high. Season and lightly
grease all meats with vegetable oil. Cook each meat to your liking.

Meanwhile, cook beans in a small saucepan of boiling salted
water for 6 minutes.

Arrange grilled meats on centre of 2 dinner plates, top with 2 slices
of butter and pile beans on the side. Serve with Tomato Jam.

This takes me back to when I started my
apprenticeship in 1979 in a busy grill restaurant at
Bayswater Road, London – and boy, did that teach you
how to cook meat! I've really enjoyed re-introducing
this old classic with the addition of Jane's amazing
Tomato Jam. The parsley butter will keep in the freezer
for weeks. Jeremy.

**To serve two people**

250g unsalted butter, softened

1 garlic clove, crushed

½ bunch flat-leaf parsley, leaves
    picked, washed and finely chopped

sea salt

freshly ground white pepper

vegetable oil

2 small minute steaks

2 sausages

4 rashers eye bacon

2 lamb's kidneys, cleaned

2 lamb cutlets

100g French beans, topped
    and tailed

2 serves Tomato Jam (see recipe
    on page 10)

## Confit of Duck Leg with Cabbage, Carrots and Bacon

Two days prior to serving, place duck in a dish and sprinkle with rock salt. Cover and refrigerate overnight. The next day, preheat oven to 180°C. Rinse duck, pat dry with paper towel and place in a baking dish with the berries, thyme, garlic, peppercorns and bay leaf. Cover with duck fat, place in oven and bring fat to a low simmer. Reduce heat to 140°C and cook for 2 hours or until duck is tender. The fat should simmer gently, never boil. Remove from oven, set aside to cool and refrigerate overnight.

Take 50g of duck fat from marylands and heat in a heavy-based saucepan over medium heat. Add onion, garlic and bacon, season and sweat until onions are soft. Add carrot and cook for 2–3 minutes. Add cabbage and white wine. Cover with a lid and cook gently, stirring occasionally, until cabbage and carrot are soft. Season to taste and keep warm.

Preheat oven to 200°C. Meanwhile, remove duck from fat and scrape away majority of fat. Place duck, skin side down, in a non-stick ovenproof frying pan, place in oven and cook for 12 minutes or until skin is crispy.

Divide cabbage between 2 large soup plates, top with duck, skin side up, and serve.

Confit is a wonderful thing to master as it will last in the fridge for weeks. The best time to make it is during some spare time over the weekend and, once cooked, it makes for a very quick weekday meal. It's wonderful served on salad if you prefer something less rich. Be careful not to overheat the fat, as the meat will overcook and go stringy. Canned duck fat can be purchased from specialty food stores or, if you are feeling really keen, you can ask your butcher for raw duck fat and render it yourself. Jeremy.

**To serve two people**

½ medium brown onion, finely sliced
1 garlic clove, finely sliced
100g bacon, cut into ½ x 3cm pieces
sea salt
freshly ground white pepper
1 carrot, cut into ½ x 3cm pieces
½ savoy cabbage, stalks removed, roughly diced into 4cm pieces
250ml white wine

**Confit of Duck Leg**

2 duck marylands, trimmed
1 tablespoon rock salt
6 juniper berries
2 sprigs thyme
3 garlic cloves
1 teaspoon black peppercorns
1 bay leaf
600g canned duck fat

## Scotch Fillet Steak Sandwich

Preheat a barbecue or frying pan on medium heat. Add a little oil and onion. Season and fry quickly until onion is dark brown but still slightly undercooked. Remove from heat and set aside.

Grill bread on both sides and spread 1 side of each slice with mustard. Season steaks and grill to your liking.

Top 2 slices of bread with meat, season well, then top with lettuce and tomato and drizzle with dressing. Pile on onions and top with remaining bread slices.

Cut in half and serve.

Unfortunately for me, steak sandwiches conjure up unpleasant memories of cooking room service in five-star hotels, but this is still quite possibly my favourite sandwich to eat. Jeremy.

**To serve two people**

vegetable oil

1 large Spanish onion, finely sliced

sea salt

freshly ground white pepper

4 slices sourdough bread

grain mustard

2 x 150g scotch fillet steaks, flattened

2 cos lettuce leaves, washed and trimmed

2 roma tomatoes, thinly sliced lengthways

Basic Salad Dressing (see recipe page 54)

## Chocolate and Hazelnut Pudding

To make pastry cream, whisk egg yolks, sugar and flour in a large bowl until well combined.

Warm milk in a medium-sized, heavy-based saucepan and pour into mixture. Mix well and return to saucepan. Cook gently on medium-low heat, stirring constantly with a whisk, for 20 minutes or until mixture has thickened.

Remove from heat, pass through a fine strainer into a bowl or plastic container. While still hot, cover surface of cream with cling film to prevent a skin from forming. Set aside until needed.

Preheat oven to 160°C. Grease two 150ml ramekins with butter or canola oil.

Combine all dry ingredients, including remaining sugar and flour, in a bowl. Make a well in centre, add egg white and stir with a spoon.

Add 125ml pastry cream and keep mixing until well combined and comes together. Spoon into moulds until 4/5 full. Bake for 30 minutes or until puffed up and slightly cracked on top.

Remove from oven, set aside to cool and then run a knife around edges of moulds to loosen puddings. Transfer to a cooling rack.

Serve on their own at room temperature or heated in a microwave and accompanied with ice-cream and chocolate sauce.

## Quick Chocolate Sauce

Bring 100ml cream to the boil. Pour over 100g chocolate buttons or chopped-up chocolate, and stir until smooth. Pour over the puddings.

These puddings are surprisingly low in fat and incredibly moist. They have a brownie-like consistency. You can't go wrong with chocolate and hazelnuts. I sometimes omit the cocoa from this recipe and serve the puddings with poached quince and quince gelati. Jane.

**To serve two people**

100g caster sugar

20g plain flour

55g hazelnut meal

50g almond meal

1 teaspoon baking powder

20g cocoa

1 egg white

**Pastry cream**

120g egg yolks

100g caster sugar

40g plain flour

500ml milk

*Note: Leftover pastry cream will keep in the fridge for 5 days and can be used as a quick dessert another time – for example, folded with some whipped cream and served with fresh berries or cake.*

## Pear Fritters with Brown Sugar, Cinnamon and Pecan Parfait

Line a 15 x 20cm tray with cling film or greaseproof paper and grease lightly with oil.

To make Cinnamon and Pecan Parfait, whisk cream to medium peaks and set aside. Place sugar and 50ml water in a small saucepan and stir over low heat until sugar dissolves. Turn heat to high and bring sugar to 115°C.

Meanwhile, whisk egg whites to medium peaks in a mixer. Try to time it so the sugar and egg whites are ready at the same time. Slowly pour sugar over egg whites while whisking. Turn mixer to high and whisk until whites are cool. Using a spatula, fold through cream, pecans and cinnamon until well incorporated. Spoon into tray and place in freezer overnight to set.

To poach pears, place all ingredients (except pears) and 500ml water in a saucepan large enough to fit liquid and pears snugly. Bring to the boil, add pears and cover with greaseproof paper and a lid or plate that fits inside the saucepan and will keep the pears submerged. Bring back to the boil, then reduce heat and simmer for 15–20 minutes, depending on the firmness of the pears. Boil one more time and cover saucepan with a lid. Remove from heat and stand for at least 30 minutes. This will finish off the poaching gently, leaving you with perfectly poached pears.

To make the batter, mix together all dry ingredients in a bowl. Whisk in beer until smooth.

To cook fritters, heat enough vegetable oil in a deep-fryer or a heavy-based saucepan to 180°C. Drain pears on paper towel, then coat in batter and deep-fry for 3–4 minutes or until golden brown. Transfer to paper towel and keep warm.

Remove parfait from freezer and turn out onto a chopping board. Cut 2 pieces from parfait and place one piece each in 2 bowls. Top with pears, sprinkle with a little brown sugar, and serve.

Reserve remaining parfait well covered in freezer to serve later.

Most parfaits are made with caster sugar. Using brown sugar adds depth and colour. It's also refreshing to not use something so refined as caster sugar. Parfaits are a great alternative to making ice-cream if you don't have an ice-cream churner. It keeps in the freezer for a few weeks. Jane.

### To serve two people

**Cinnamon and Pecan Parfait**

300ml cream (35% fat content)

140g brown sugar, plus extra for sprinkling

2 egg whites

100g pecans, roughly chopped

2 teaspoons ground cinnamon

**Poaching Liquor**

250ml white wine

250g white sugar

½ cinnamon stick

1 clove

½ star anise

½ lemon rind

2 beurre bosc pears (or other firm brown pears), peeled, halved, core removed

**Batter**

1 cup self-raising flour

1 teaspoon salt

1 tablespoon caster sugar

¾ cup beer

vegetable oil, for deep frying

## Strawberry and Rosewater Granita
## with Vanilla Ice-cream

Bring 200ml water and sugar to the boil in a saucepan. Remove from heat and allow to cool. Once cold, add strawberry puree and pass mixture through a fine strainer. Add a few drops rosewater to taste. Pour into a 20 x 10cm tray and place in freezer.

Once frozen, scrape granita with a fork to create fine shards of ice. Place a scoop of ice-cream in the bottom of 2 bowls or glasses. Top with granita and serve immediately.

Perfect for eating on a summer's day, this granita has so much flavour and a surprising amount of body. It is also one of the simplest desserts to make and among the most impressive you'll ever serve. I sometimes serve it with a piece of baklava on the side. Jane.

**To serve two people**

100g caster sugar
100ml (about 1 punnet)
  strawberry puree
rosewater
good-quality vanilla ice-cream

## Spiced Pumpkin Pie with Nutmeg Cream

Preheat oven to 160°C.

Cut pastry in half and roll out to 2.5mm thick on a lightly floured bench. Line two 8cm-diameter tartlet shells with pastry, then cover with foil and top with rice or pastry weights. Place in oven and blind bake for 10–15 minutes or until golden brown. Remove weights and foil and brush with 1 egg yolk. Return to oven and bake for another 2 minutes.

Preheat oven to 125°C. Whisk together 2 egg yolks and sugar. Bring cream to the boil and pour over yolks. Add pumpkin and spices and pass through a conical strainer.

Pour mixture into the baked tartlet cases and bake in oven for 10–20 minutes or until just set. Transfer to a cooling rack. When cool enough to handle, remove pies from tartlet shells and place on 2 dessert plates.

To make Nutmeg Cream, lightly whisk cream with nutmeg and sugar. Serve on the side.

Pumpkin is one of my favourite vegetables and is wonderful roasted or made into a soup. Its sweet nutty flavour lends itself well to this dessert – another, less common, way of using pumpkin. Jeremy.

### To serve two people

150g sweet pastry
3 egg yolks
20g caster sugar
165ml cream (35% fat content)
80g pumpkin puree
1 pinch nutmeg
1 pinch cinnamon

### Nutmeg Cream
100ml pure cream (45% fat content)
1 pinch nutmeg
1 teaspoon caster sugar

## Peach and Mascarpone Trifle

Bring wine, 700ml water and caster sugar to the boil in a saucepan that will fit the liquid and peaches snugly. Add peaches and bring back to the boil. Cover with greaseproof paper and a lid or a plate that fits inside the saucepan and will keep the peaches submerged. Simmer gently for 10 minutes. Bring back to the boil and cover with a lid.

Remove from heat and stand for at least 30 minutes. Remove peaches and gently peel off skin, then cut in half and discard seeds. Cut each half into 6 pieces. Pass poaching syrup through a fine strainer, and reserve 400ml.

Stir icing sugar and a tablespoon of poaching liquor through mascarpone until smooth. Soak gelatin leaves in cold water. Bring reserved poaching syrup to the boil and add softened gelatin leaves. Set aside to cool.

Crush 2 sponge biscuits and place 1 each in the bottom of 2 tumblers. Sprinkle with some vodka. Cover each biscuit with 6 peach slices. Pour over some cooled poaching syrup to just cover peaches. Place in fridge.

Once jelly has set, cover each with a layer of mascarpone (using half of mascarpone). Place 1 crushed sponge biscuit on top of each mascarpone layer. Sprinkle with vodka. Place remaining peach slices on top and just cover with poaching syrup. Allow to set in the fridge.

Cover with remaining mascarpone and smooth to the edges before serving.

Poaching peaches can be tricky as they are such delicate fruits. This method is the best I've ever used, so you should have success. These trifles can be made a few days in advance. The poaching liquor is delicious and has a beautiful pink hue. Try using it in a cocktail with lots of vodka and some poached peach slices as garnish. Jane.

**To serve two people**

400ml white wine
400g caster sugar
2 large peaches
40g icing sugar
150g mascarpone
3 gelatin leaves
4 sponge biscuits
vodka

## Lemon and Vanilla Panna Cotta in Blueberry Soup

Warm the milk, vanilla bean, seeds and lemon rind in a saucepan over medium heat and allow to infuse off the heat for 15 minutes. Add sugar and allow to dissolve over medium heat.

Soak gelatin in cold water and, when soft, squeeze out excess water and add to warm milk. Pass mixture through a fine strainer and allow to cool. Stir in cream and pour into 2 lightly greased 150ml plastic dariole moulds. Refrigerate overnight.

To make Blueberry Soup, bring 200ml water and sugar to the boil. Add 300g blueberries and simmer gently for about 10 minutes to allow flavour and colour to 'come out' of blueberries. Pass through a fine strainer. Chill and add gin.

Turn panna cottas out of moulds onto the centre of 2 bowls. Surround with remaining blueberries, pour around soup and serve.

You will be amazed at how much colour and flavour come out of the blueberries, giving this dessert its striking appearance. Jane.

**To serve two people**

140ml milk

½ vanilla bean, split, seeds
   scraped and reserved

rind of ½ lemon

50g caster sugar

2 gelatin leaves

140ml cream (35% fat content)

**Blueberry Soup**

150g caster sugar

400g blueberries, washed

30ml gin

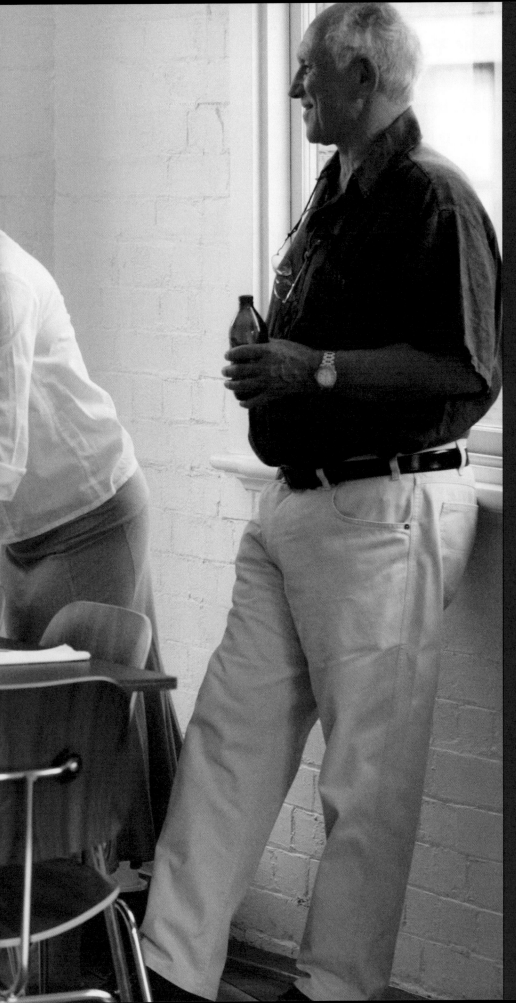

# Fridays for four.

Friday night is the start of the weekend, so why not start to unwind with a couple of friends over for dinner? These recipes involve a little more planning and preparation, but they are still easy to achieve to create two- or three-course meals. Whatever the menu, sharing a meal is a lovely way to end the week. If your guests are close friends or family, they could even help in the kitchen!

## Potted Pork

The day before cooking, place the meat and fat on a tray and rub lightly with salt. Cover and refrigerate overnight.

Preheat oven to 130°C. Cut the meat and fat into roughly 3cm cubes. Place in an oven dish with the remaining ingredients. Add 100ml water, season with pepper and cover with a lid. Place over medium heat and bring to the boil. Place in the oven and cook for at least 3 hours or until meat is completely soft and simmering in its own fat.

Remove from the oven and season to taste (make sure the pork has plenty of salt, as something so fatty will taste extremely bland if under-seasoned). Drain the mixture through a colander into a large bowl and allow to cool slightly. Remove the bay leaf and thyme stalks.

Beat the mixture lightly with a large spoon for 1 minute, then stir with a fork to achieve a stringy texture. Divide the meat between four 150ml ramekins and cover with fat, leaving behind any juices. Cover with cling film or foil and refrigerate until set.

Remove ramekins from fridge at least 20 minutes before serving to allow pork to soften slightly. Place on a plate with a few tiny gherkins on the side and serve with sourdough toast.

This is an old reliable I've cooked throughout my career, in restaurants and bistros and cafes. The French call it rillettes and it's sometimes made with duck or rabbit. You'll need some spare time to make this, maybe over a weekend. It keeps in the fridge for up to 2 weeks and it's great to have around for canapés, a snack or even a picnic or barbecue.
Jeremy.

**To serve four people**

300g pork belly
300g pork neck
300g pork fat
2 sprigs thyme
1 bay leaf
1 garlic clove, peeled
sea salt
freshly ground black pepper

## Salt Cod Fish Cakes with Herb Mayonnaise

Completely cover fish with rock salt, leaving no flesh exposed. Refrigerate for 2 days. Wash off salt and soak in cold water overnight.

Place fish in a saucepan and cover with milk. Add bay leaf, onion, thyme and garlic and bring to the boil. Remove from heat and allow to cool. Remove fish and flake with a fork.

Place fish, potato and olive oil in a food processor and blend until fish and potato just come together (do not over-blend). Season with pepper. Remove from processor, divide into 4 equal portions and press into a 5cm-diameter ring or cutter. Whisk eggs and milk in a bowl. Dust each cake lightly in flour, dip in egg mixture and coat with breadcrumbs.

Heat a deep-fryer with vegetable oil to 180°C. Fry fish cakes for 3 minutes or until golden brown. Drain on paper towel.

To make Herb Mayonnaise, mix herbs with mayonnaise and season to taste.

Serve with Herb Mayonnaise on the side and salad leaves.


I've been making a version of 'brandade' (a blend of salt cod and olive oil) for many years. Turning it into fish cakes, bread crumbing and deep frying has been a recent adaptation. A single large fish cake makes a great accompaniment to a roasted piece of fish for a main course, while bite-size cakes are perfect as canapés. Jeremy.

### To serve four people

1 x 400g fillet blue eye, skin on

rock salt

1L milk

1 bay leaf

¼ brown onion

1 sprig thyme

1 garlic clove

150g potato, boiled, passed through a mouli

100ml extra-virgin olive oil

freshly ground white pepper

2 free-range eggs

50ml milk

200g flour

200g breadcrumbs

vegetable oil, for deep frying

### Herb Mayonnaise

2 sprigs dill, leaves picked and chopped

½ bunch chives, finely chopped

4 sprigs parsley, leaves picked, washed and chopped

6 tablespoons mayonnaise

sea salt

## Red Mullet with Couscous Salad
## and Burnt Orange Vinaigrette

Combine orange juice, olive oil, ¼ teaspoon pepper, cardamom, bay leaf and eschalots together in a bowl. Lay fish in a dish, pour over marinade and refrigerate for 1 hour. Remove mullet and pat dry on paper towel. Reserve marinade.

To make the vinaigrette, heat sugar in a saucepan over high heat. As sugar starts to melt and colour, lift and swirl pan around so sugar melts evenly. Allow sugar to go almost black in colour. Carefully add marinade to sugar (it will spit and splutter). Reduce heat to low and allow sugar to dissolve. Season to taste with salt to balance the sweetness. Pick out bay leaves and cardamom pods.

To make Couscous Salad, place couscous and butter in a bowl and season. Bring water or stock to the boil, pour over couscous, stir and cover with a lid. Stand for 5 minutes. Remove lid and stir well to fluff up couscous. Allow to cool, stir through remaining ingredients, dress with some vinaigrette and season to taste.

Place a little vegetable oil in a cold, non-stick frying pan, season mullet and place in pan, skin side down. Fry on medium heat for 3 minutes or until skin is golden brown. Gently turn over and cook for another 30 seconds.

Divide Couscous Salad among 4 dinner plates. Top each with 2 fillets and drizzle with a little Burnt Orange Vinaigrette.

Making a dressing out of burnt sugar and orange juice may sound a little odd, but it works. I'm not sure how the idea popped into my head and was a little dubious when I first tried it myself. Mullet and orange are fantastic together and whenever this dish is on the menu, it's a hit. Jane.

**To serve four people**

200ml orange juice

80ml olive oil

freshly ground white pepper

3 cardamom pods

2 bay leaves

6 eschalots, finely sliced

8 x 80g fillets red mullet, skin on, boned

⅓ cup caster sugar

sea salt

vegetable oil

**Couscous Salad**

100g couscous

10g unsalted butter

5 tablespoons water or stock

2 tablespoons raisins, soaked in a strong cup of tea until plump, drained

8 sprigs coriander, leaves picked and finely shredded

8 sprigs parsley, leaves picked and finely shredded

4 tablespoons pine nuts, toasted

## Grilled Quail, Lentil and Verjuice Salad

Preheat an open grill or barbecue. Season quails, brush with vegetable oil and grill each side for 5 minutes.

Meanwhile, heat a frying pan over medium heat. Add olive oil and bacon and cook for 3 minutes. Remove from heat, allow to cool slightly, add verjuice and season.

Place salad leaves, lentils, bacon and verjuice dressing in a bowl and toss to combine. Place equal quantities on the centre of 4 plates.

Drizzle remaining lentils and dressing around leaves and top with quails.

We would serve this salad as a slightly refined dish, with the breasts and legs of the quail removed from the bone. Verjuice complements all white meats and fish. You can use a good-quality vinegar as an alternative, but you only need half the amount, as the flavour of verjuice is more subtle. Jeremy.

### To serve four people

4 quails, butterflied

sea salt

freshly ground white pepper

vegetable oil

50ml olive oil

2 rashers bacon, rind removed, cut into ½cm strips

20ml verjuice (or 10ml vinegar)

1 small handful wild rocket, washed

1 small handful baby beetroot leaves, washed

1 small handful watercress, leaves picked and washed

4 sprigs flat-leaf parsley, leaves picked and washed

6 sprigs chervil, leaves picked and washed

30g Puy lentils, boiled in water or chicken stock until soft, drained

*Note: To butterfly quail, remove backbone and flatten.*

*Puy lentils are small green lentils from the French region of Puy. In Australia they are now called Australian French-style lentils, because of regional recognition laws. They are available at specialty food shops.*

## Snapper with Spiced Capsicum Stew, Coriander and Labna

To make the Spiced Capsicum Stew, heat 4 tablespoons olive oil in a heavy-based saucepan over medium-low heat. Add onion and garlic, season and sweat onions until soft. Add ground spices and cook, stirring, for 5 minutes. Add capsicum, chilli and sugar and simmer for 15 minutes or until capsicum is soft. Season to taste.

Heat a little vegetable oil in a non-stick ovenproof frying pan over medium heat. Season snapper and place in pan, skin side down. Fry for 2 minutes or until golden brown. Turn over and cook for a further 2 minutes. Turn again, place pan in oven and roast for 5 minutes or until just cooked.

Place a tablespoon of labna in the middle of 4 large soup plates. Place equal portions of Spiced Capsicum Stew around each labna portion. Top with snapper.

Mix lemon juice and remaining olive oil in a bowl. Add coriander and preserved lemon. Toss together gently and place equal portions on top of each snapper fillet.

The Spiced Capsicum Stew is based on harissa (a hot paste used in North African cuisine) and contains similar ingredients. We first put this on the menu at Sydney's MG Garage. All the flavours work wonderfully together, which makes this dish exciting to eat and look at. Jane.

**To serve four people**

vegetable oil

4 x 200g fillets snapper, skin on, boned

4 tablespoons labna

1 teaspoon lemon juice

½ bunch coriander, washed, leaves picked

¼ preserved lemon, flesh removed and discarded, rind finely sliced

**Spiced Capsicum Stew**

5 tablespoons olive oil

1 medium brown onion, diced into ½cm pieces

2 garlic cloves, finely chopped

sea salt

freshly ground white pepper

¼ teaspoon ground cumin

¼ teaspoon ground coriander

½ teaspoon ground fennel

3 red capsicums, diced into 1cm pieces

1 red chilli, finely chopped

1 teaspoon caster sugar

*Note: See recipe for labna on page 58.*

## Steamed Barramundi with
## Prawn Dumplings and Beef Broth

To make Beef Broth, place stock, lime leaf, chilli, ginger and lemongrass in a saucepan and bring to the boil. Reduce heat and simmer for 10 minutes. Set aside to infuse.

Meanwhile, to make Prawn Dumplings, combine prawns and coriander in a bowl. Season with a few drops of sesame oil and sea salt. Lay wonton wrappers on a lightly floured bench. Place even quantities of prawn mixture on the centre of each wonton. Brush sides with a little water and fold wrappers over to seal. Blanch wontons in a saucepan of boiling water for 1 minute, refresh in iced water until cold, and set aside. Drizzle with a little vegetable oil to prevent wontons sticking.

Strain Beef Broth and season with soy sauce, rock sugar and a few drops sesame oil.

Place barramundi in a steamer and steam for 8 minutes or until just cooked. Reheat prawn dumplings in steamer for 3 minutes. Steam or boil Asian greens until just cooked.

Place fish in 4 large soup bowls, top each with 3 dumplings and place greens alongside. Pour over hot broth.

Barramundi is a great fish to steam as it has lots of flavour. I love this dish because it is both clean and hearty. The beef broth makes a great meal on its own with steamed greens, sliced shiitake mushrooms and bean shoots. Jane.

### To serve four people

4 x 200g fillets barramundi, skin on, boned

2 bunches Asian greens (bok choy, Chinese broccoli or Vietnamese watercress), washed

### Prawn Dumplings

250g green prawns, peeled and chopped finely or minced

½ bunch coriander, washed, leaves picked and roughly chopped

sesame oil

sea salt

12 wonton wrappers

vegetable oil

### Beef Broth

500ml beef stock

1 kaffir lime leaf

1 long red chilli, seeds removed

½ knob ginger, roughly sliced

1 stalk lemongrass, trimmed

soy sauce

rock sugar (see note)

*Note: Rock sugar, or rock candy, is sugar cane and water traditionally processed to rock-like crystals. It is available from most Asian grocery stores but can be substituted with white sugar or light palm sugar.*

## Roast Rack of Lamb with Roast Potatoes, Asparagus and Mint Hollandaise

Preheat oven to 200°C.

Bring potatoes to the boil in salted water and drain. Heat a roasting tray over medium heat and add a little vegetable oil. Add potatoes, season and place in oven. Cook for 40 minutes or until golden brown and soft inside.

Meanwhile, season lamb racks. Heat another roasting tray over medium heat, add a little vegetable oil and cook seasoned lamb on both sides for 3 minutes. Place tray in oven, with lamb fat side down, and cook for 20 minutes (to medium-rare) or to your liking. Remove from oven, cover with foil and set aside to rest in a warm place.

To make Mint Hollandaise, place peppercorns in a small saucepan with the vinegar and boil until reduced by half. Pass through a fine strainer and place in a bowl with egg yolks. Add a dash of water and place saucepan over 3cm of simmering water in another saucepan. Whisk continuously until yolks have tripled in volume and leave a trail when whisk is lifted. Turn off heat. Slowly add olive oil in a steady stream, whisking continuously. Stir in a squeeze of lemon juice and mint and season to taste. Remove from heat and sit in a warm place.

Cook asparagus in boiling salted water for 3–4 minutes, then drain.

Carve lamb between each bone and divide among 4 dinner plates. Arrange asparagus and potatoes beside lamb. Spoon Mint Hollandaise over lamb and asparagus, and serve.

As lamb, mint and olive oil make such good partners, it occurred to me to make a hollandaise out of olive oil instead of butter. This resulted in a lighter meal. Asparagus and lamb have always married well and spring is the perfect time for them. Jeremy.

### To serve four people

4 small desiree potatoes, peeled, quartered

vegetable oil

sea salt

freshly ground white pepper

2 x 6-boned lamb racks, French-trimmed

16 medium asparagus spears, peeled, trimmed

### Mint Hollandaise

½ teaspoon white peppercorns, crushed

3 tablespoons white-wine vinegar

2 egg yolks

250ml olive oil

½ lemon

¼ bunch mint, leaves picked and chopped

## Pork Chop with Braised Red Cabbage
## and Kipflers Fried in Duck Fat

Preheat oven to 150°C.

Heat 100g butter in a medium-sized, heavy-based saucepan over medium heat. Add onion, garlic and apples, season and sweat until onions are soft. Add cabbage, vinegar and wine. Cover with a well-greased circle of greaseproof paper and bring to the boil. Place in oven and braise, stirring every 15 minutes so cabbage cooks evenly and edges don't catch, for 1 hour or until soft.

Meanwhile, peel potatoes and cut diagonally into 1cm-thick slices. Remove cabbage from oven, season to taste and keep warm.

Turn oven up to 180°C. Heat a non-stick ovenproof frying pan with a little vegetable oil over medium heat. Season pork chops and cook on one side for 4 minutes. Turn over, add remaining butter and roast in oven, turning once, for 6 minutes or until firm to the touch. Remove from pan and keep warm.

Meanwhile, heat duck fat in a separate non-stick frying pan over medium heat. Add potatoes and season. Fry each side for 3 minutes or until deep golden brown. Transfer to a paper towel.

Divide cabbage among 4 large plates, top with pork chops, place potatoes alongside and serve.

As with all ingredients, it's important to buy the best available within your budget. Ask your butcher for good-quality pork – we use Bangalow Sweet Pork from northern New South Wales. You really will taste the difference. We use kipfler potatoes in lots of ways; they are especially good for frying as they are waxy and hold together well. Duck fat can be substituted in this recipe with clarified butter or oil, but will not have the same richness after the potatoes are cooked. Jeremy.

### To serve four people

140g unsalted butter

2 small brown onions, finely sliced

4 garlic cloves, finely sliced

2 red apples, skin on, finely sliced

sea salt

freshly ground white pepper

1 small red cabbage, shredded

100ml red-wine vinegar

1L red wine

8 large kipfler potatoes, boiled
    with skin on

vegetable oil

4 x 200g pork chops

4 tablespoons duck fat

## Passionfruit Delicious Pudding

Preheat oven to 180°C.

In a large bowl mix 70g sugar, egg yolks, juices and butter with a spoon until smooth. Sift in flour and bicarbonate of soda. Add milk and mix until smooth.

Whisk egg whites in a mixer, gradually adding remaining sugar, until stiff peaks form. Using a whisk, combine egg whites with egg-yolk mixture. Pour evenly into four 200ml ramekins. Place on a baking tray and fill tray to 3cm deep with cold water. Bake in oven 30–40 minutes or until puddings are light golden brown on top and puffed up.

Serve with cream or custard.

Lemon Delicious Pudding is the classic dessert, but passionfruit makes for a pleasant change. Although passionfruit is high in acid, you still need to add lemon juice to create the curd at the bottom. This will always be one of my favourite desserts. Jane.

**To serve four people**

140g caster sugar

3 egg yolks

60ml seedless passionfruit juice

2 teaspoons lemon juice

50g unsalted butter, melted

45g plain flour

1 pinch bicarbonate of soda

260ml milk, brought to
    room temperature

2 egg whites

# Baked Vanilla Custard in Fig and Port Soup

Preheat oven to 130°C.

Whisk together eggs and 25g sugar in a bowl until just combined. Place the milk, vanilla bean and seeds and remaining sugar in a saucepan, bring to the boil and pour immediately over egg-and-sugar mixture. Mix well and pass through a fine strainer. Pour into 4 lightly greased plastic dariole moulds. Place on a baking tray and fill with hot water until moulds are half immersed. Bake in oven for 40 minutes or until custards are just set. Remove from oven and set aside to cool. Refrigerate until ready to serve.

To make Fig and Port Soup, preheat oven to 160°C. Place 6 figs, orange rind and juice, cinnamon quill, honey and 100ml water in a baking tray. Cover with foil and bake in the oven for 1 hour.

Meanwhile, bring sugar and 60ml water to the boil and set aside. Place port in a saucepan and boil until reduced by half. Add sugar syrup and bring to the boil again. Remove baking tray from oven, set figs aside and pour liquid through a fine strainer into a bowl. Puree figs in a blender, pass through a fine strainer and add to baking liquid. Add port and place soup in refrigerator until chilled.

Remove custards from refrigerator and carefully run a thin knife around edges to loosen. Invert on to centre of 4 soup bowls. Cut remaining 4 figs into 6 segments each and arrange evenly around custards.

Pour over soup and serve.

We're fans of soups as desserts. They are a light end to a meal and are impressive when poured at the table. Jane.

## To serve four people

2 free-range eggs
50g caster sugar
250ml milk
½ vanilla bean, seeds scraped

## Fig and Port Soup

10 figs
rind and juice of 1 orange
½ cinnamon quill
1 teaspoon honey
80g caster sugar
300ml port

## Orange and Campari Crème Brûlée
## with Orange Salad

Preheat oven to 115°C.

Heat the orange juice in a saucepan on medium heat until reduced to 20ml. Set aside to cool.

Meanwhile, whisk the egg yolks and sugar together well in a medium-sized bowl. Add the orange juice and Campari. Pour the cream and milk into a saucepan, bring to the boil and pour immediately over the egg mixture. Whisk until fully combined, then pass through a fine strainer.

Pour custard into four 150ml ramekins. Place ramekins on a baking tray and fill tray with hot water until ramekins are half immersed. Cover tray tightly with foil and bake in oven for 1 hour or until brûlées are just set. Remove ramekins, set aside to cool and refrigerate.

To make Orange Salad, remove zest from oranges and place in a saucepan with the sugar and Campari. Cut the oranges into segments, reserving as much of the juice as possible, and place in a bowl. Add juice to saucepan and bring to the boil to dissolve sugar. Pour syrup over orange segments and refrigerate.

Sprinkle brûlées with a thin, even layer of sugar right to the edge. Place ramekins under a grill on high, or use a blowtorch, until sugar is a deep golden brown.

Serve with Orange Salad on the side.

The creaminess of this brûlée is balanced by the tartness of the orange salad. Brûlées can feel heavy if eaten on their own. Campari and orange are a classic combination and the bitterness of the Campari adds to the complexity of flavours in this dessert. Jane.

**To serve four people**

200ml orange juice, reduced to 20ml

8 egg yolks

60g caster sugar, plus extra for sprinkling

2 tablespoons Campari

300ml pure cream (45% fat content)

100ml milk

**Orange Salad**

2 large oranges

100g caster sugar

2 teaspoons Campari

## Milk Chocolate Mousse with Almond Toffee

Whisk the cream to medium peaks and set aside. Melt the chocolate in a bowl over a saucepan of gently simmering water and set aside. In a mixer whisk the yolks until they form a ribbon-like consistency when the whisk is lifted.

Meanwhile, place 50ml water and the sugar in a saucepan and bring to 115°C. Pour slowly over eggs while whisking and whisk for another 3 minutes. Pour chocolate down side of bowl while whisking eggs on slow speed, then whisk on high speed for 3 minutes. Whisk in a third of the cream.

Remove bowl from mixer and scrape down sides. Return to mixer and, once cream is fully incorporated, whisk in another third of cream. Remove bowl from mixer and fold through remaining cream with a spatula. When completely mixed in, pour into four serving glasses and refrigerate overnight to set.

To make Almond Toffee, place sugar and a dash of water in a clean, heavy-based saucepan and heat over low heat, stirring constantly, until sugar dissolves. Increase heat to high and, just swirling pan to cook evenly (do not stir), bring mixture to 160°C or until dark caramel in colour. Add almonds and stir to combine.

Pour toffee onto a baking tray lightly sprayed with oil, spread evenly with a spoon and put aside to set. Place on a chopping board and cut into small pieces.

Sprinkle toffee over mousse and serve.

There are plenty of chocolate mousse recipes around, but I have found this one to be consistently good and versatile. You can set it in a container and then, using a piping bag, fill any number of pastry creations. I like to use it in profiteroles instead of pastry cream when making a *croquembouche*. It can also be used to mask cakes and then decorate with chocolate curls. Serve with fresh berries, when they are in season, instead of the toffee. Jane.

### To serve four people

760ml thickened cream

500g Callaubaut dark chocolate, or any other good quality dark cooking chocolate

10 egg yolks

200g sugar

### Almond Toffee

200g sugar

100g slivered almonds, lightly toasted

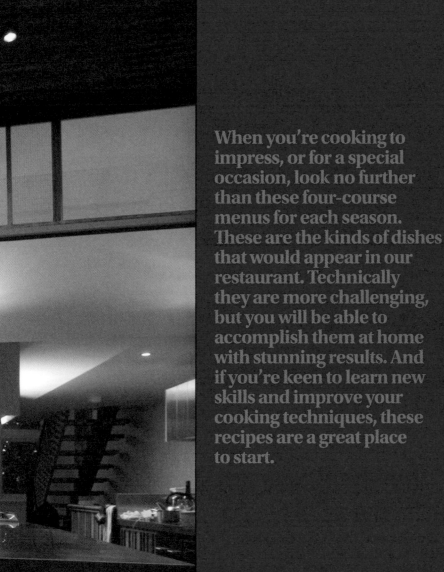

# Big night in.

When you're cooking to impress, or for a special occasion, look no further than these four-course menus for each season. These are the kinds of dishes that would appear in our restaurant. Technically they are more challenging, but you will be able to accomplish them at home with stunning results. And if you're keen to learn new skills and improve your cooking techniques, these recipes are a great place to start.

To help you, we have written a work plan for each menu so that you don't spend the whole day and night in the kitchen. We've included all the steps you can complete before your guests arrive. As most of the dishes require finishing or cooking just before serving, there will still be a few steps to carry out. We haven't included these in the work plans as they are explained in each recipe. The aim of the work plans is to help you achieve a smooth and efficient lead-up to your dinner party – it's important that you enjoy a relaxed evening as much as your guests.

# Big night in.
# A note on menu balancing

When planning an unforgettable feast for your friends or family, the hardest part can be working out how the courses will fit together. We've put together four-course menus for each season to show how balancing works.

The thought of putting together a dinner party can be daunting, so we've also provided a plan of action at the beginning of each menu to help you cook up a storm, enjoy the day's preparation, and be relaxed when your guests arrive.

**Do not repeat ingredients throughout your menu.** That way, each dish will be fresh and different from the last.

**Create seasonal menus.** The seasons will determine what's available and affect how much you feel like eating and at what temperatures it is best to serve different courses. For example, a chilled soup is perfect to start a summer dinner party, but you wouldn't serve a chilled dish in winter.

**Balance flavours and textures.** Each course should fit in with other courses, so one does not overpower the experience of next course. We've made sure each course has its own balance of richness, acidity, savouriness and sweetness. We've also ensured that a very sweet course doesn't follow another sweet course, a highly acidic course doesn't follow another acidic course, and so on. Texture is always very important. Food quickly becomes boring when all the textures are the same. The feeling we get in our mouths is as important as the flavours we are experiencing.

**Portion size** is another consideration for successful menu planning. The greater the number of courses, the smaller each course should be. This enhances the dining experience, because you can experience a wider range of flavours and cooking methods.

**Vary your cooking methods.** For example, you wouldn't serve two or three fried courses in a four-course menu.

**Balance ingredients.** We always make a point of balancing meat and seafood throughout our menus. For example, if you have a rich main course based on meat, you would serve two fish, or one fish and one vegetarian, entrée so that the whole meal isn't too heavy. It's also a good idea to serve a light dessert after a rich meal and a richer dessert or cheese after a light meal.

**Presentation** is a major factor in menu planning. Vary the colours, shapes and sizes of each dish.

**Salad suggestion.** A green salad at the end of the main course refreshes your palate before dessert. Use the Basic Salad Dressing on page 54.

At the end of a balanced meal, no guest will feel either too full or hungry. Each course will excite and satisfy in its own way and leave your guests in anticipation of the next great dinner party.

# Spring
from page 140

Rabbit, French Bean and
   Hazelnut Salad
Crab Raviolo and Crushed
   Peas with Crab and
   Tarragon Vinaigrette
Roast Fillet of Snapper,
   Asparagus Puree and
   Dauphine Potatoes
Cheese Plate with Oatcakes

**Make in the morning**
Crab stock
Raviolo dough and filling
Cut rabbit
Make dough for Oatcakes
Dauphine Potato mixture
Asparagus Puree

**Make in the afternoon**
Rabbit salad preparation
Rabbit salad dressing
Crushed Peas
Pick tarragon
Bake Oatcakes

**Just before guests arrive**
Make raviolo
Shape Dauphine Potatoes
Make Crab and Tarragon
Vinaigrette

# Summer
from page 150

Jellied Quail Consommé
Smoked Eel with Cauliflower
   Panna Cotta
Roasted Veal Rack with Baby
   Spinach Puree, Braised
   Onions and Madeira Gravy
Banana Fritters with
   Tropical Fruit Salad
   and Coconut Soup

**Make the day before**
Quail stock
Cauliflower Panna Cotta

**Make in the morning**
Witlof marmalade
Braised Onions
Fritter dough
Coconut Soup

**Make in the afternoon**
Clarify consommé
Cook quail eggs
Cut eel
Spinach Puree

**Just before guests arrive**
Cook quail breasts
Roast veal
Cut fruit

# Autumn
from page 160

King George Whiting
   Rollmops with Beetroot
   Compote
Ocean Trout with Cabbage
   and Sweet Pork
Loin of Venison with
   Celeriac Puree and
   Chocolate Sauce
Autumn Fruits with
   Red Wine Jelly

**Make the day before**
Pickle King George
whiting fillets
Make Red Wine Jelly
Poach fruit

**Make in the morning**
Base for Chocolate Sauce
Cook pork hock
Beetroot Compote
Tuile mixture

**Make in the afternoon**
Celeriac Puree
Whiting dressing
Cook cabbage
Remove pork from bone
Bake tuiles
Mascarpone filling

**Just before guests arrive**
Drain whiting

# Winter
from page 170

Warm Parsley Soup
   with Oysters
Warm Duck Confit, Calamari
   and Lentil Salad
Guinea Fowl Breast
   with Turnip Gratin
   and Silverbeet
Maple Syrup and Lime Tart
   with Crème Fraiche Sorbet

**Make the day before**
Start Confit Duck Leg
Pastry

**Make in the morning**
Confit Duck Leg
Blind bake tart shell
Tart filling
Crème Fraiche Sorbet
Prepare guinea fowl
Roast guinea fowl bones
Guinea fowl sauce

**Make in the afternoon**
Bake tart
Cook lentils
Wash silverbeet
Salad garnish
Calamari
Segment orange

**Just before guests arrive**
Turnip gratin
Parsley Soup

## Rabbit, French Bean and Hazelnut Salad

Prepare rabbit by removing hind legs and loins. Discard front legs and carcass. Remove as much sinew as possible. (You should be able to get your butcher to do this for you.) Preheat oven to 180°C.

Add cracked wheat to a small saucepan of salted boiling water and cook for 20 minutes or until soft. Drain.

Heat a little vegetable oil in an ovenproof frying pan over medium heat. Season rabbit legs and cook for 2 minutes each side or until golden, to seal. Add half the butter, place pan in oven and cook for 10 minutes. Remove rabbit from pan and set aside to rest in a warm place. Repeat this process for the loin but cook 30 seconds each side, without colouring, to seal gently, and cook in oven for 3 minutes. Remove loin from pan and rest with the legs.

To make dressing, whisk together hazelnut oil and sherry vinegar in a small bowl and season. Place beans in salted boiling water, cook for 6 minutes, then immediately place in cold water, to refresh. Halve beans lengthways and place in a bowl with curly endive, watercress, cracked wheat and hazelnuts. Trim 1cm from base of witlof, separate leaves and add to salad.

Cut the main sections of leg meat from the bone and carve into thin slices. Add to salad. Carve each loin diagonally into 9 pieces.

Season salad lightly and pour over dressing. On 6 individual plates arrange 3 witlof leaves in a circle. Place a piece of loin on each leaf. Pile the remaining salad in the centre of each plate and sprinkle with any remaining cracked wheat.

Wine recommendation: Viognier

In spring, we want to serve lighter meals. Farmed white rabbit is a great product – it's lean, clean-tasting and not heavy. The cracked wheat and hazelnuts add body and texture. Hazelnut oil gives greater depth of flavour than olive oil, and we've kept the dressing light by not adding mustard. French beans add colour and crunch.

### To serve six people

1 x 1.5kg rabbit, skinned, cleaned

30g coarse cracked wheat

vegetable oil

sea salt

freshly ground white pepper

20g unsalted butter

50ml hazelnut oil

10ml sherry vinegar

150g French beans, trimmed

1 small head curly endive, trimmed, pale leaves retained and washed

½ bunch watercress, leaves picked and washed

75g hazelnuts, roasted, peeled, lightly crushed

3 heads witlof

*Note: Coarse cracked wheat, coarse grit and coarse burghul are available at health-food stores and some supermarkets. Sherry vinegar can be found at specialty stores; red-wine vinegar makes a good substitute.*

## Crab Raviolo and Crushed Peas
## with Crab and Tarragon Vinaigrette

To make Crab and Tarragon Vinaigrette, preheat oven to 200°C. Using a large knife or cleaver, roughly chop blue swimmer crab and place in a roasting tray. Drizzle with vegetable oil, place in oven and roast for 30 minutes.

Meanwhile, heat some vegetable oil in a heavy-based saucepan over medium heat, add carrot, onion and celery and fry for 4 minutes. Add garlic, coriander seeds and peppercorns. Reduce heat to low, add tomato paste and cook, stirring regularly, for another 5 minutes or until golden brown. Add wine, increase heat to high and cook until liquid is reduced by three-quarters. Add blue swimmer crab, fish stock, thyme, tarragon stalks and bay leaf and bring to the boil. Skim off any impurities, reduce heat to low and simmer for 1 hour and 15 minutes. Remove from heat and pass through a fine strainer into a clean saucepan. Cook until mixture is reduced to around 100ml. Set aside.

To make pasta dough, place flour and salt in a food processor and process for a few seconds. Add egg, yolks and a drizzle of olive oil and pulse until dough comes together. Transfer dough to a lightly floured bench and knead for 5 minutes or until smooth. Wrap in cling film and rest for at least 30 minutes.

Meanwhile, place blue eye in clean food processor and pulse for 30 seconds. Add egg white and pulse for a further 30 seconds. Scrape mixture from side and pour in cream slowly while processing. Stop processor, season well with salt and cayenne pepper, scrape mixture from sides and pulse for 30 seconds. Remove fish mousse to a bowl, add picked crab meat and refrigerate.

Set a pasta machine to its widest setting. Cut dough in half, pass it through once, drop setting by one, pass through again, and repeat process. Lay pasta on bench and fold into 3. Return pasta machine to widest setting and repeat this whole process twice. Now that you have laminated the dough, take it down gradually to the smallest setting. Use as little flour as possible when rolling and cut into shorter lengths as the pasta gets long and harder to handle. Repeat for remaining dough to taste. Lay a tea towel over rolled-out pasta to prevent drying out.

Cut six 6cm-diameter circles and six 8cm-diameter circles. Spoon crab-and-cream mixture evenly onto the centre of the smaller circles. Brush edges lightly with water. Place larger circles on top and press down edges, being careful not to leave any air pockets and maintaining a dome shape. Place on a lightly floured tray.

To make Crushed Peas, cook peas in a saucepan of boiling salted water for 2 minutes. Drain, add butter and season. Using a hand blender, blend to a coarse mixture, and season to taste. Set aside and keep warm.

Warm crab stock in a small saucepan. Chop tarragon leaves and add to stock. Whisk in 1 tablespoon olive oil and lemon juice to taste. Cook the raviolo in a large saucepan of boiling salted water for 4 minutes.

Place a spoonful of pea mash in the centre of 6 individual plates. Lift ravioli carefully out of water with a slotted spoon and place on top of mash. Drizzle with vinaigrette and serve immediately.

Wine recommendation: Chablis

**To serve six people**

250g plain flour
1 teaspoon table salt
1 egg
125g egg yolks
olive oil
150g blue eye or other white fish, roughly chopped
1 egg white
150ml cream (35% fat content)
sea salt
1 pinch cayenne pepper
250g fresh, picked crab meat
300g fresh or frozen peas
20g unsalted butter
freshly ground white pepper

**Crab and Tarragon Vinaigrette**

1 small whole blue swimmer crab, cleaned, guts and gills removed
vegetable oil
1 carrot, peeled, diced
½ small brown onion, diced
1 stick celery, washed, diced
2 garlic cloves
1 teaspoon coriander seeds
1 teaspoon white peppercorns
1 tablespoon tomato paste
150ml white wine
1L fish stock
3 sprigs thyme
½ bunch tarragon, leaves picked, stalks reserved
1 bay leaf
juice of ½ lemon

After the well-textured rabbit salad, it's nice to move onto something smooth and silky, such as a raviolo. Tarragon and shellfish are a common partnership and this viniagrette is more like a sauce.

## Roast Fillet of Snapper, Asparagus Puree and Dauphine Potatoes

Preheat oven to 200°C. Preheat a deep fryer to 170°C (see note).

To make Dauphine Potatoes, bring butter, milk, 125ml water, salt and sugar to the boil in a medium-sized, heavy-based saucepan. Add flour and mix in vigorously. Cook over medium heat until mixture starts to come away from sides of saucepan. Remove saucepan from heat and beat in eggs, one at a time. Cook potatoes in salted boiling water, peel and pass through a mouli.

Measure out 500g of dough and add 500g potato. Mix well and season to taste. Using two dessertspoons and some boiling water for dipping, make 6 egg-shaped dumplings. Rest each on a strip of greaseproof paper.

To make Asparagus Puree, cut off asparagus tips, leaving 5cm-long stalks, and reserve 18 tips. Roughly chop stalks. Melt butter in a saucepan on medium-low heat. Add onion, season and sweat until soft. Add chopped asparagus and pour in enough stock or water to almost cover asparagus. Simmer until very soft and liquid has reduced. Using a jug or hand blender, puree until very smooth. Pass through a conical strainer and season to taste. Set aside and keep warm.

Heat a little vegetable oil in a non-stick ovenproof frying pan over high heat. Season snapper and place in pan, skin side down. Cook for 2 minutes or until golden brown. Turn over and cook for a further 1 minute. Turn again, skin side down, and place in oven for 5 minutes or until fish is just cooked. Remove from pan, set aside and keep warm.

Meanwhile, drop Dauphine Potatoes into deep fryer and cook for 7 minutes or until golden brown and puffed up. Cook reserved asparagus tips in boiling salted water for 4 minutes or until tender.

Place a large spoonful of Asparagus Puree on 6 plates. Top with a snapper fillet, then a Dauphine Potato and place 3 asparagus tips alongside. Season to taste and serve immediately.

Wine recommendation: barrel-fermented Sauvignon Blanc

Spring is the best season for asparagus. It brings acidity, texture and colour, while the Dauphine Potatoes deliver richness and salt. Snapper has a wonderful texture, especially when roasted until the skin is crispy.

**To serve six people**

vegetable oil

6 x 150g fillets snapper, skin on, bones removed

**Dauphine Potatoes**

100g butter

125ml milk

1 teaspoon salt

1 teaspoon caster sugar

170g flour

4 eggs

800g desiree potatoes

freshly ground white pepper

**Asparagus Puree**

3 bunches asparagus, trimmed, peeled

25g unsalted butter

1 small brown onion, finely sliced

sea salt

freshly ground white pepper

250ml chicken stock or water

olive oil

*Note: If you don't have a deep fryer, place 2L of good cooking oil, such as canola or cottonseed, in a large, heavy-based saucepan and heat carefully over medium heat to 170°C. Monitor the heat with a high-range thermometer or sugar thermometer. Make sure the oil does not fill the saucepan by more than two thirds.*

## Cheese Plate with Oatcakes

To make Oatcakes, combine 50g rolled oats and all other dry ingredients in a large bowl. Using your fingertips, rub in butter to form fine crumbs. Add milk and mix to form a soft dough. Cover with cling film and rest in the fridge for 30 minutes.

Preheat oven to 160°C. Roll out dough to just over ½cm thickness. Using a round 4cm-diameter cutter, cut out shapes and place on a non-stick baking tray. Sprinkle each cake with remaining oats. Bake in oven for 15 minutes or until light golden brown. Transfer to a cooling rack.

Cut each cheese into 6 even slices and allow to come to room temperature. Place 1 slice of each cheese on 6 plates with 3 oatcakes to the side.

Wine recommendation: aged Semillon, or red if you prefer

After three rather light courses, cheese is a good option. Spring is perfect for fresh cheese, as spring milk is full of all those wonderful grassy flavours. A fresh goat's cheese is perfect. When choosing cheeses to be served together it's important to balance their individual tastes and textures. This is why we've chosen a soft fresh cheese; a mature, hard and sharp cheese; and a heady blue cheese. Serving muscatels and/or quince paste helps cut their richness. Some people prefer to use fresh fruit, or even celery, to achieve the same result.

**To serve six people**

200g Australian fresh goat's cheese
200g mature English cheddar
200g French blue cheese

**Oatcakes**
70g rolled oats
350g flour
80g raw sugar
1 teaspoon sea salt
2 teaspoons baking powder
150g unsalted butter, softened
milk

## Jellied Quail Consommé

The day before serving, preheat oven to 200°C. Remove breasts from quails and place carcasses and chicken wings on a roasting tray. Drizzle with a little vegetable oil and roast in oven for 30 minutes or until golden brown.

Heat a little vegetable oil in a heavy-based saucepan over medium heat. Add carrot, onion and celery and fry for 8 minutes or until golden brown. Add garlic and peppercorns halfway through cooking. Add thyme, bay leaves, roasted bones and stocks. Bring to the boil, skim off any impurities, reduce heat and simmer for 1 hour and 15 minutes. Skim off impurities now and again. Pass through a fine strainer, leave to cool and refrigerate.

The next day, remove from refrigerator and scrape any fat and impurities off the top. Place the egg whites in a deep saucepan and half-whisk. Add quail stock and whisk well. Place saucepan over a medium flame and bring to the boil slowly, whisking regularly to make sure mixture doesn't catch on the bottom and burn. As mixture comes to the boil, do not whisk again, and reduce heat to low. The egg whites will rise to the surface with most of the impurities to clarify the stock. The egg whites will firm and form a 'raft' on the surface. Make a hole in the raft with a kitchen spoon and season to taste. Leave to simmer for 15 minutes to allow the raft to catch any remaining impurities.

Remove from heat and, using a ladle, gently pour the finished consommé through a fine strainer lined with muslin, or a clean, wet tea towel, into a clean container. Cool and refrigerate to allow the consommé to jelly.

Bring a small saucepan of water to the boil and cook quail eggs for 2 minutes and 20 seconds. Refresh in iced water. Very carefully peel and place in clean, cold water.

Heat a frying pan over medium heat and add butter. Season quail breasts, add to pan and cook, skin side down, for 3 minutes. Reduce heat to low, turn over breasts and cook for a further 3 minutes. Remove from pan and allow to cool. Slice in half on a slant.

Remove consommé from fridge and break up slightly with a whisk. Place a spoonful of jelly in the centre of 6 bowls and top with half a breast and half an egg. Drizzle with olive oil, season and serve.

Wine recommendation: Beaujolais

**To serve six people**

3 quails

500g chicken wings, roughly chopped up

vegetable oil

1 carrot, peeled, sliced into ½cm-thick pieces

1 brown onion, diced into 1cm pieces

1 celery stick, washed, diced into 1cm pieces

2 whole garlic cloves

1 teaspoon black peppercorns

3 sprigs thyme

2 bay leaves

1L chicken stock

1L veal stock

5 egg whites

sea salt

freshly ground white pepper

3 quail eggs

10g butter

olive oil

*Note: Ask your butcher to order quail eggs for you. Alternatively, they are available from specialty grocers or David Jones Food Hall.*

A chilled soup is an obvious choice in summer. This jellied consommé has a clean yet meaty flavour. You could make this in one day, but you would need to chill the quail stock in an ice bath before clarifying, as a far better result is achieved.

## Smoked Eel with Cauliflower Panna Cotta

To make Cauliflower Panna Cotta, lightly grease six 4 x 7cm rectangular plastic containers with canola spray or vegetable oil.

Place cauliflower in a saucepan, just cover with water and simmer until water has almost evaporated. Pour over stock to just cover, season well and simmer again until cauliflower is completely soft and stock is reduced by two-thirds. Using a jug or bar blender, puree until very smooth and reserve 250ml of puree.

Warm the milk in a clean saucepan. Soften gelatin in cold water and add to milk. Add milk to puree and allow to cool. Add cream and season to taste. (Cold foods need more seasoning than warm foods). Pour evenly into each container and allow to set in the fridge for at least 2 hours, preferably overnight.

To make the witlof marmalade, place eschalots, saba and vinegar in a small saucepan and reduce over medium-high heat to a syrup. In another saucepan, melt butter over medium heat and add witlof. Season and cook until witlof releases liquid. Add vinegar syrup and sugar and cook gently for 10 minutes. Season to taste and set aside to cool.

Cut head off eel and discard. Cut body into 6 even sections. Peel off skin and, using a small thin knife and staying close to the backbone, cut off a fillet from each side. Allow eel to come to room temperature.

Gently tip panna cottas onto the centre of 6 plates. They should just slide out of their moulds. Mix parsley and chives through witlof marmalade. Using a spoon and your fingers, spread some marmalade onto the top of each panna cotta and top with 2 fillets of eel. Season and serve.

Wine recommendation: Chardonnay

Smoked eel is wonderfully rich and voluptuous. Its flavour is intense and earthy. It is best served at room temperature. The panna cotta is smooth and creamy, while the witlof and saba add acid, bite and texture. After the clean, yet full-flavoured consommé, your palate is ready for something richer. If you don't fancy eel, you can substitute it with smoked trout fillets.

### To serve six people

2 eschalots, finely diced

25ml saba

2 teaspoons red-wine vinegar

15g unsalted butter

2 heads witlof, halved lengthways, core removed, finely sliced

sea salt

freshly ground white pepper

2 tablespoons brown sugar

1 smoked eel

6 sprigs flat-leaf parsley, leaves picked, finely chopped

¼ bunch chives, finely chopped

*Note: Saba is a concentrate made from grape must. It can be found at specialty food stores. A sweet, well-aged balsamic is a good substitute.*

### Cauliflower Panna Cotta

¼ large cauliflower, core removed, finely sliced

chicken stock

125ml milk

2½ x 2g gelatin leaves

125ml pure cream (45% fat content)

## Roasted Veal Rack with Baby Spinach Puree, Braised Onions and Madeira Gravy

To make Braised Onions, heat a heavy-based saucepan over medium heat, add 100g butter and melt. Add sugar, dissolve, then add onions and cook, stirring regularly, for 6 minutes or until onions are caramelised and a deep golden brown. Add vinegar and reduce to a syrup. Add 400ml veal stock, bring to the boil, season lightly and simmer for 20 minutes or until just cooked. Remove from heat and keep warm.

Preheat oven to 180°C. Heat a roasting tray over high heat. Add a little vegetable oil and 100g butter and allow to colour slightly. Add the meat and cook on all sides until golden brown. Stand meat upright, season, place in oven and roast for 20 minutes per kilo.

Meanwhile, to make Baby Spinach Puree, blanch spinach for 2 minutes in a saucepan of boiling salted water. Drain and squeeze out as much excess water as possible. Place in a jug blender with 30g butter and plenty of seasoning and puree until very smooth. Place in a clean, small saucepan.

Remove meat from roasting tray and rest in a warm place for at least 15 minutes. Drain off excess fat, return to medium heat, add Madeira and cook until reduced by half. Add stock, reduce by half again and pass through a fine strainer into a clean saucepan and keep hot.

Reheat the spinach puree and the onions. Carve the rack between the bones into 6 cutlets and place one in the centre of 6 warm dinner plates. Place 2 onions to the side of the veal. Drizzle the veal and the plate with some gravy, top the veal with a spoonful of puree, and serve.

Wine recommendation: Cabernet Sauvignon

You are now ready for a warm dish after two cooling starters. We've chosen veal, as it is a lighter meat than beef or lamb. The spinach puree has a velvety texture and adds colour and earthiness. Vinegar in the braised onions gives this dish its acidity and sweetness. Madeira and veal are a classic combination and the gravy is kept light in keeping with the entire meal.

### To serve six people

330g unsalted butter

1 tablespoon caster sugar

12 pickling onions, peeled, with tops and bottoms remaining

70ml red-wine vinegar

850ml veal stock

sea salt

freshly ground white pepper

vegetable oil

1 x 6-bone rack of veal, French trimmed

600g baby spinach, washed and leaves picked

200ml Madeira (Malmsey)

*Note: Due to regional recognition laws in Australia, Madeira is now called Malmsey, one of the grape varieties that Madeira is produced from. It is available from most liquor stores.*

## Banana Fritters with Tropical Fruit Salad and Coconut Soup

Bring butter, milk, 125ml water, salt and sugar to the boil in a medium-sized heavy-based saucepan. Add flour and cook until mixture starts to come away from the sides of pan. Remove from heat and beat in eggs, one at a time. Set aside to cool, then refrigerate.

To make Coconut Soup, bring 125ml water and sugar to the boil. Remove from heat, allow to cool and add all other ingredients. Allow to infuse for 1–2 hours. Pass through a fine strainer and refrigerate.

Preheat a deep fryer to 170°C. Mix banana into dough and, using two dessertspoons, shape dough into walnut-sized dumplings and drop into deep fryer. Fry for 5–6 minutes or until golden brown. For 6 serves, you will need to fry 18 fritters. Place cooked fritters on some paper towel in a low-heat oven to keep warm.

Arrange fruit to one side of 6 soup plates. Dust fritters with caster sugar and place beside fruit. Pour Coconut Soup over fruit and around bowl.

Wine recommendation: Botrytis Gewurztraminer

There's no better time to eat tropical fruit than in summer. This dessert marries hot and cold, acid and creaminess, richness and cleanness. The fresh fruit has texture and acidity, the coconut soup is creamy, the fritters are hot and rich. This is a refreshing way to finish the meal.

### To serve six people

100g butter

125ml milk

1 teaspoon salt

1 tablespoon caster sugar, plus extra for sprinkling

170g flour

4 eggs

250g ripe banana, mashed with a fork

tropical fruits (such as mango, lychee, mangosteen, passionfruit and dragon fruit), sliced

### Coconut Soup

125g caster sugar

2 lemongrass stalks, trimmed, crushed

1 knob ginger, peeled, sliced

½ star anise, warmed in oven to refresh

1 kaffir lime leaf, torn

500ml Kara coconut cream

*Note: Kara coconut cream is homogenised and a far superior product to use for this particular recipe. It doesn't separate like other canned coconut creams and has a stunning white colour. It's available in tetra packs from most Asian supermarkets.*

## King George Whiting Rollmops
## with Beetroot Compote

To make the rollmops, the day before serving bring all ingredients (except whiting and watercress) and 300ml water to the boil and allow to cool. Roll whiting from tail end tightly and secure with a toothpick. Place in pickling mixture and refrigerate overnight.

To make Beetroot Compote, heat the olive oil in a heavy-based saucepan over medium-low heat. Add onion and garlic, season well and sweat until very soft. Add beetroot, vinegar and mustard seeds, increase heat to medium and cook for 15 minutes or until beetroot is al dente. Season to taste, remove from heat and set aside to cool before placing in a container.

To make the dressing, place egg yolk in a bowl and whisk in the mustard. Gradually add olive oils, whisking constantly to emulsify (as for mayonnaise). Whisk in 50ml of the whiting pickling mixture, then the cream and season.

Place a tablespoon of Beetroot Compote at the six o'clock position on 6 medium-sized plates. Remove whiting fillets from the pickling mixture, drain on paper towel and remove toothpicks. Place on top of compote. Place a small pile of watercress at the twelve o'clock position on each plate and drizzle dressing in a circular motion around whiting and over the watercress.

Wine recommendation: Marsanne

Pickled whiting has a clean flavour with plenty of acidity from the pickling liquor. For this reason, a course high in acidity is a great way to start a meal, as acid stimulates your tastebuds. The beetroot adds colour, texture and earthiness. The creamy dressing balances the acidity – without it, the dish would be too sharp.

### To serve six people

300ml white-wine vinegar

300g caster sugar

1 teaspoon fennel seeds

1 tablespoon yellow mustard seeds

4 sprigs thyme

1 bay leaf

6 x 100g King George whiting fillets, boned

½ bunch watercress, sprigs picked and washed

### Beetroot Compote

100ml olive oil

1 medium brown onion, finely chopped

2 garlic cloves, finely chopped

sea salt

freshly ground white pepper

2 large beetroots, peeled, coarsely grated

60ml white-wine vinegar

1 teaspoon yellow mustard seeds

### Dressing

1 egg yolk

1 tablespoon grain mustard

100ml extra-virgin olive oil

100ml virgin olive oil

25ml cream (35% fat content)

## Ocean Trout with Cabbage and Sweet Pork

Preheat oven to 200°C.

Melt the butter a heavy-based saucepan over medium-low heat. Add onion and garlic, season and sweat for 12–15 minutes or until very soft. Add cabbage and white wine and cook slowly with a lid on, stirring occasionally, for 30 minutes or until cabbage is soft. Season to taste and set aside.

Place palm sugar and 1 tablespoon of water in a frying pan and cook over medium heat until sugar dissolves. Increase heat to high and cook until sugar turns a golden caramel. Add pieces of hock, lower heat and allow to cook 5 minutes. Remove hock from caramel and add to cabbage.

Heat a non-stick ovenproof frying pan with a little vegetable oil on medium heat. Season trout, place in pan, skin side down, and cook for 2–3 minutes or until golden brown. Turn over and place in oven for 2 minutes.

Reheat cabbage and place a few dessertspoonsful in the centre of 6 medium-sized plates. Top with trout, skin side up, and serve.

Wine recommendation: Semillon

The cabbage and sweet pork are rich and unctuous. There are savoury and sweet flavours at play in this dish and the full-flavoured trout copes well with the cabbage. Due to the acidity in the cabbage, there is a nice progression from the whiting to the venison, the richness building but not in direct contrast. Make sure to cook the trout skin until it is crispy to give this dish its texture. This is a great meal on its own.

**To serve six people**

50g unsalted butter

1 small brown onion, finely sliced

1 garlic clove, finely chopped

sea salt

freshly ground white pepper

¼ savoy cabbage, finely sliced

250ml white wine

50g palm sugar, chopped

1 small ham hock (cooked as in recipe on page 47)

vegetable oil

6 x 75g fillets ocean trout, skin on, boned

## Loin of Venison with Celeriac Puree and Chocolate Sauce

Preheat oven to 200°C.

Place celeriac in a small saucepan with 50g butter and 150ml water. Season and bring to the boil. Reduce heat to a simmer and cook until very soft. Add cream and cook gently for 10 minutes.

Meanwhile, heat a little vegetable oil in a medium-sized saucepan over medium heat. Lightly fry eschalots until slightly coloured. Add half the pepper, then berries, coriander, vinegar and wine. Cook for 10–12 minutes or until reduced to a syrup. Add brown stock and thyme. Bring to the boil, skim any impurities from surface and cook for 20–25 minutes or until liquid is reduced to a sauce-like consistency. Pass through a fine strainer into a clean saucepan and set aside.

Using a jug or bar blender, puree celeriac until very smooth. Season to taste and keep warm.

Heat a small amount of vegetable oil in a frying pan over medium heat. Season venison with salt and remaining pepper. Sear lightly on all sides and add half the remaining butter. Place in oven and roast for 3 minutes on each side. Remove from pan and rest in a warm place. Heat another frying pan over medium heat and add remaining butter. When butter is foaming add spinach, season and fry until just wilted. Drain on paper towel.

Re-boil the sauce, whisk in chocolate and season to taste. Carve each venison loin in half and spread out to the sides of 6 warmed dinner plates. Spoon a tablespoon of celeriac puree onto the plates. Evenly divide spinach between plates. Spoon some sauce over the venison and around the plate.

Wine recommendation: Shiraz

As venison is a rich meat, we have chosen two fish dishes to begin the meal. Game is traditionally served in autumn and we like to keep to these traditions. Venison is very lean, so we have served rich garnishes. The celeriac is velvety in texture and arrives in autumn. There's sweetness from the sweet potato and the small amount of chocolate in the sauce is more mysterious than overpowering. The vinegar in the sauce gives a small amount of acidity to cut the rich meat and sauce. Spinach adds colour and texture.

### To serve six people

1 medium celeriac, peeled, diced into 2cm pieces

100g unsalted butter

sea salt

freshly ground white pepper

100ml cream (35% fat content)

vegetable oil

3 eschalots, finely sliced

1 tablespoon black peppercorns, crushed

4 juniper berries, crushed

½ teaspoon coriander seeds, crushed

20ml red-wine vinegar

250ml red wine

800ml brown stock, reduced to 400ml

1 sprig thyme

6 x 200g portions of venison loin, trimmed, denuded

250g baby spinach, washed, trimmed

10g dark chocolate, grated

## Autumn Fruits with Red Wine Jelly

Bring 125ml water and sugar to the boil, then remove from heat. Place wine in a separate saucepan and cook over medium-high heat until reduced by half. Add sugar syrup, cardamom, cinnamon, peppercorns, clove, star anise and lemon rind, bring to the boil, then remove from heat. Allow to infuse for at least a few hours, overnight if possible.

Pass poaching liquid through a fine strainer into a clean, medium-sized saucepan. Bring to the boil and add pears and apples. Reduce heat and simmer for 1 minute. Add rhubarb, cover with a lid and then set aside so that rhubarb cooks in remaining heat in pan. Once cooled, place in fridge to chill.

Remove fruit gently from liquor. Soak gelatin leaves in cold water to soften. Bring poaching liquid back to the boil and add gelatin. Pass through a fine strainer and place in a tray or container and allow to set in fridge. Reserve a small amount of liquor to store poached fruit.

To make the tuiles, preheat oven to 130°C. Cream butter and sugar in a mixer until light and fluffy. Add egg whites slowly. Once fully incorporated, fold through flour and cinnamon. Using a palette knife, spread mixture onto a lightly greased non-stick tray, or a greaseproof paper-lined tray, in six 8 x 8cm squares. Bake in oven for 12–16 minutes or until a pale golden brown colour. Quickly peel tuiles off tray and, going diagonally across, roll each around a thick-handled wooden spoon or a cannelloni stick. Transfer to another dish and repeat process. If tuiles become too stiff to mould, return to oven briefly to soften. Mix together mascarpone, brown sugar and hazelnuts. Place in a piping bag with a small nozzle and pipe into tuiles.

Remove jelly from fridge and break up with a spoon. Divide evenly in 6 flat soup plates. Arrange 2 pieces of each fruit on top. Garnish with mascarpone-filled tuiles.

Wine recommendation: sparkling red

This jelly is slightly astringent and refreshing to the palate. It's also not too filling. Apples and pears are best in autumn. The tuiles and hazelnuts add texture, and the mascarpone brings richness to the dish without being overly sweet.

### To serve six people

140g caster sugar

750ml red wine

2 cardamom pods

8 black peppercorns

1 clove

½ cinnamon stick

1 star anise

rind of ½ lemon

2 beurre bosc pears, each cut lengthways into 6 pieces, core removed

2 royal gala apples, each cut into 6 wedges, core removed

3 sticks rhubarb, each cut into 12 even lengths

3 gelatin leaves

### Tuiles

50g butter, softened

65g sugar

65g egg whites, at room temperature

55g plain flour

2 pinches ground cinnamon

350g mascarpone

20g brown sugar

30g hazelnuts, roasted, peeled, roughly chopped

## Warm Parsley Soup with Oysters

Melt the butter in a saucepan over low heat. Add the onion, leek and celery, and sweat until soft. Add 1L water and potato and bring to the boil. Season and reduce heat to a simmer.

Meanwhile, blanch the parsley in a saucepan of boiling salted water for 15 seconds, then refresh in a bowl of iced water. Drain and squeeze out excess water.

When potato is fully cooked, remove from heat, add parsley and blend quickly until very smooth. Pass through a conical strainer into a clean saucepan and season to taste. Keep hot, but do not overheat.

Place oysters in the centre of 6 small soup plates. Pour soup around oysters and serve.

Wine recommendation: Riesling

Oysters are at their peak in winter, so it's the best time to eat them. Parsley and oysters go well together as they both have a very slight metallic taste. Oysters are high in zinc and parsley is high in iron. The colour of this soup is incredible and the flavour clean and fresh – the perfect start to any dinner party.

**To serve six people**

30g unsalted butter

20g brown onion, finely chopped

20g leek, finely chopped, washed

20g celery, finely chopped, washed

125g potato, peeled, diced finely

sea salt

freshly ground white pepper

200g flat-leaf parsley, leaves picked and washed

18 small Pacific oysters, shucked

## Warm Duck Confit, Calamari and Lentil Salad

Heat a saucepan over medium heat and add half the olive oil.
Add onion, celery, carrot and garlic. Season well, reduce heat
to medium-low and sweat vegetables until very soft.

Meanwhile, place lentils in a saucepan of cold water. Bring to the
boil, then drain immediately. Add lentils, bay leaf, thyme and stock
to soft vegetables. Simmer gently for 20–25 minutes or until lentils
are soft. Season to taste and set aside.

Remove duck leg from fat and, using your fingers, shred the
meat, discarding bone and skin. Heat a non-stick frying pan with
a little vegetable oil over high heat. Season calamari and sauté
for 3 minutes. Add duck to pan and cook for 1 minute. Drain on
paper towel.

Mix together lemon juice and remaining olive oil. Toss watercress
and shiso with lemon dressing.

Place lentils in the bottom of each soup plate. Add duck and
calamari to salad and toss quickly. Arrange evenly on top of lentils.

Wine recommendation: Chardonnay

In winter, you can handle a richer meal. The fatty duck
confit works well with the crunchy calamari, while the
lemon dressing adds acidity and the lentils add texture
and earthiness. Peppery watercress and purple shiso
give colour, crunch and bite. Mixing meat and seafood
always makes for interesting eating.

**To serve six people**

80ml olive oil

½ medium brown onion, finely diced

½ celery stick, finely diced

½ carrot, finely diced

1 garlic clove, finely diced

sea salt

freshly ground white pepper

75g Puy lentils

1 bay leaf

3 sprigs thyme

500ml beef stock

1 confit duck leg (see recipe on
    page 96)

vegetable oil

3 small calamari bodies, cleaned,
    cut into 1cm strips

2 teaspoons lemon juice

1 bunch watercress, picked and washed

1 punnet baby purple shiso, picked
    and washed

## Guinea Fowl Breast with Turnip Gratin and Silverbeet

Preheat oven to 200°C.

Remove legs from guinea fowls, cut in half and set aside. Using a heavy knife, cut around base of wing next to breast, turn knife over and tap wing bone firmly just in front of the first joint. Pull end of wing firmly and you'll have a clean piece of wing bone, attached to the breast, for presentation. Carefully remove breasts from carcass, ensuring fillets remain attached to the breast. Trim skin, leaving enough to just cover the flesh, and put to one side. Chop carcass into 6 pieces. Place in a roasting tray with the legs and drizzle with vegetable oil. Roast in oven for approximately 40 minutes or until golden brown.

Meanwhile, heat a deep saucepan over medium heat and add a dash of vegetable oil. Add carrot, onion and celery and fry until golden brown. Halfway through cooking, add garlic, berries and peppercorns. Remove meat from tray and add to the vegetables.

Drain excess oil from tray, place on medium heat, add wine and cook until reduced by half. Pour into saucepan, scraping off all caramelisation from bottom and cook until reduced by half again. Add stock, thyme, bay leaf and a pinch of salt. Bring to the boil, skim away any impurities, reduce heat and simmer for 1 hour and 15 minutes, skimming now and again.

Pour orange juice in a clean saucepan over medium heat and cook until reduced by half. Pass the guinea fowl stock through a fine strainer into the juice and cook for 20–30 minutes or until reduced to a sauce-like consistency. Season to taste and set aside.

Meanwhile, to make Turnip Gratin, reduce oven temperature to 150°C. Grease a small gratin dish with a little butter. Using a mandolin, finely slice the potatoes and turnips to 2mm thick. Place a layer of potato in the bottom of the dish, half overlapping each slice. Repeat with the turnip and season lightly. Repeat this process until potato and turnip are used up. Season the cream, bring to the boil in a saucepan and pour into the gratin dish. Once settled, the cream should just cover the potato and turnip. Place in oven and bake for 50 minutes or until potatoes and turnips are soft and golden brown on top. Remove from oven and keep warm.

Return oven to 200°C. Heat an ovenproof frying pan over medium heat and add half the butter. Heat the butter, but do not colour. Add the seasoned breasts, skin side down, and cook for 1 minute. Turn over and cook for 1 minute, return to skin side, cover with foil and place in oven for 5 minutes – the breast should be slightly pink under the fillet. Remove from oven and pan and keep warm.

Heat a saucepan over medium heat, add remaining butter and a dash of water. Add silverbeet, season, cover with a lid and cook for 5 minutes. Drain and keep warm.

Cut the orange segments into 3, bring sauce to the boil and add orange.

Divide the gratin between 6 large, warm plates. Cut the breast in half widthways and on a slant and place on top of gratin. Place the silverbeet at the twelve o'clock position on the plates and pour sauce over guinea fowl.

Wine recommendation: Grenache

### To serve six people

3 x 1kg guinea fowls

vegetable oil

1 carrot, peeled, sliced into ½cm-thick pieces

½ small brown onion, diced into 1cm pieces

1 stick celery, washed, diced into 1cm pieces

2 garlic cloves

4 juniper berries

1 teaspoon black peppercorns

250ml white wine

2L chicken stock

3 sprigs thyme

1 bay leaf

sea salt

1 blood orange, segmented, excess juice reserved

75g unsalted butter

250g silverbeet, stalks discarded, washed

freshly ground white pepper

### Turnip Gratin

2 large desiree potatoes, peeled

2 large turnips, peeled

300ml cream (35% fat content)

Heavy, braised dishes are perfect in winter, but not when you have to eat four courses. So we've opted for a bird instead. Blood oranges are excellent and have a short season, so use them when you can. The turnip gratin has bitterness and creaminess in texture and flavour and pulls this meal together.

## Maple Syrup and Lime Tart
## with Crème Fraiche Sorbet

Preheat oven to 160°C.

Roll pastry on a lightly floured bench to about ½cm thick. Line a 26cm round tart shell or a 13 x 35cm rectangular tart shell with pastry and allow to rest in fridge for at least 1 hour. Line shell with aluminium foil and fill with weights or rice. Blind bake tart shell for 25 minutes or until golden brown. Remove weights and foil and brush liberally with egg yolk. Return to oven and bake for another 5 minutes.

Reduce oven temperature to 140°C. Whisk sugar and eggs in a mixer until sugar dissolves. (Do not incorporate too much air.) Melt butter and maple syrup in a saucepan over medium heat. Add to egg mixture. Add dry ingredients and, when fully incorporated, stir through lime juice. Pour into tart shell and bake in oven for 45 minutes or until just set in the middle but still a little wobbly. Remove from oven and place on a cooling rack. When cool enough to handle, remove tart from tin.

To make Crème Fraiche Sorbet, bring 250ml water and caster sugar to the boil. Chill and mix in crème fraiche. Pass through a fine strainer. Churn in an ice-cream churner until thick and creamy.

Slice 6 wedges from the tart and place on each plate with a scoop of sorbet alongside.

Wine recommendation: Cordon Cut Riesling

This dessert has everything going on – the maple syrup is sweet, the lime juice acidic, the pastry savoury and the crème fraiche balances sweet and sour. This tart is refreshing and rich all at the same time.

### To serve six people

300g savoury shortcrust pastry

2 egg yolks

200g brown sugar

4 free-range eggs

160g unsalted butter

400g maple syrup

30g breadcrumbs

1½ tablespoons plain flour, sifted

¼ teaspoon sea salt

3 limes, juiced and strained

### Crème Fraiche Sorbet

350g caster sugar

500ml crème fraiche

*Note: If you don't have an ice-cream churner, simply serve plain crème fraiche.*

**al dente**
pasta, rice or vegetables cooked just long enough to still be firm in the centre

**blanch**
to cook in boiling water until al dente and then refresh in iced water

**blind bake**
weighting pastry with rice or other weights while baking to prevent it rising

**caramelise**
to cook until very soft and a deep golden colour

**conical strainer**
conical-shaped strainer with coarse holes

**cream, % fat content**
different creams have different fat content percentages. These can be found on product labels.

**dariole**
cup-shaped plastic mould with a capacity of about 100ml

**emulsify**
to convert the fine dispersion of one liquid into another by whisking

**fine strainer**
conical strainer with very small holes or fine mesh

**firm peaks**
refers to whipping cream or egg whites. Peaks should be very stiff and hold their shape with definite edges.

**gelatin leaves**
gelatin leaves can be found at specialty stores. They come in different strengths and it can be quite confusing choosing the right one. Gelatin leaves weighing 2–2.5g are the normal strength, sometimes called silver strength. 1 teaspoon of powdered gelatin is equivalent to 2 leaves.

**mandolin**
Japanese-style slicer used for cutting vegetables and fruit finely and evenly

**medium peaks**
refers to whipping cream or egg whites. Peaks should be in between soft and firm stages.

**mouli**
a mill that purees fruits and vegetables

**pin-bone**
to remove the tiny bones that run down the centre of a fillet of fish. Simply find the bone line with your finger, then run your finger backwards along this line to expose the bones. Using a pair of tweezers or small pliers carefully pull out the bones one by one.

**ramekin**
porcelain or china dish used for baking

**refresh**
to plunge an item into iced water to arrest cooking

**rest**
to allow meat to relax after cooking, so that juices are retained when carving and meat is more tender

**rock salt**
coarse salt in rock form

**sauté**
to pan fry, achieving some colour

**seal**
browning of meat over high heat

**season, seasoning**
sea salt and freshly ground pepper

**soft peaks**
refers to whipping cream or egg whites. Peaks should just be starting to form but not have much shape.

**sweat**
to cook slowly without colouring

**weights**
beads made from porcelain or metal used to weigh pastry down when baking

**Note**

We haven't included recipes for stocks, mayonnaise and pastry as many cookbooks include these basics.

For basic stocks we recommend *Passion for Flavour*, Gordon Ramsay (Conran Octopus).

For mayonnaise and pastry we recommend *The Cook's Companion*, Stephanie Alexander (Viking).